Principles
in Practice

The Principles in Practice imprint offers teachers concrete illustrations of effective classroom practices based in NCTE research briefs and policy statements. Each book discusses the research on a specific topic, links the research to an NCTE brief or policy statement, and then demonstrates how those principles come alive in practice: by showcasing actual classroom practices that demonstrate the policies in action; by talking about research in practical, teacher-friendly language; and by offering teachers possibilities for rethinking their own practices in light of the ideas presented in the books. Books within the imprint are grouped in strands, each strand focused on a significant topic of interest.

Adolescent Literacy Strand

Adolescent Literacy at Risk? The Impact of Standards (2009) Rebecca Bowers Sipe

Adolescents and Digital Literacies: Learning Alongside Our Students (2010) Sara Kajder

Adolescent Literacy and the Teaching of Reading: Lessons for Teachers of Literature (2010) Deborah Appleman

Writing in Today's Classrooms Strand

Writing in the Dialogical Classroom: Students and Teachers Responding to the Texts of Their Lives (2011) Bob Fecho

Becoming Writers in the Elementary Classroom: Visions and Decisions (2011) Katie Van Sluys

Writing Instruction in the Culturally Relevant Classroom (2011) Maisha T. Winn and Latrise P. Johnson

Literacy Assessment Strand

Our Better Judgment: Teacher Leadership for Writing Assessment (2012) Chris W. Gallagher and Eric D. Turley

Beyond Standardized Truth: Improving Teaching and Learning through Inquiry-Based Reading Assessment (2012) Scott Filkins

Reading Assessment: Artful Teachers, Successful Students (2013) Diane Stephens, editor

Literacies of the Disciplines Strand

Entering the Conversations: Practicing Literacy in the Disciplines (2014) Patricia Lambert Stock, Trace Schillinger, and Andrew Stock

Real-World Literacies: Disciplinary Teaching in the High School Classroom (2014) Heather Lattimer

Doing and Making Authentic Literacies (2014) Linda Denstaedt, Laura Jane Roop, and Stephen Best

Beyond "Teaching to the Test"
Rethinking Accountability and Assessment for English Language Learners

Betsy Gilliland
University of Hawai'i Mānoa

Shannon Pella
California State University, Sacramento

National Council of Teachers of English
1111 W. Kenyon Road, Urbana, Illinois 61801-1096

Staff Editor: Bonny Graham
Series Editor: Cathy Fleischer
Interior Design: Victoria Pohlmann
Cover Design: Pat Mayer
Cover Image: iStock/skynesher

NCTE Stock Number: 02947; eStock Number: 02954
ISBN 978-0-8141-0294-7; eISBN 978-0-8141-0295-4

Library of Congress Cataloging-in-Publication Data

Names: Gilliland, Betsy, 1973- author. | Pella, Shannon, 1966- author.
Title: Beyond "teaching to the test" : rethinking accountability and assessment for English language learners / Betsy Gilliland (University of Hawaii Mānoa), Shannon Pella (Sacramento City Unified School District).
Description: Urbana, IL : Urbana, Illinois : National Council of Teachers of English, [2017] | Includes bibliographical references and index.
Identifiers: LCCN 2017003098 (print) | LCCN 2017023795 (ebook) | ISBN 9780814102954 | ISBN 9780814102947 (pbk.) | ISBN 9780814102954 (eISBN)
Subjects: LCSH: English language—Study and teaching—Foreign speakers.
Classification: LCC PE1128.A2 (ebook) | LCC PE1128.A2 G5256 2017 (print) | DDC 428.0071—dc23
LC record available at https://lccn.loc.gov/2017003098

Contents

Acknowledgments

We are especially grateful to the teachers who feature in this book. Talia, Gary, Rachel, Elizabeth, and Laura opened up their classrooms and engaged enthusiastically in discussions of language, literacy, teaching, and learning. So many other teachers have shared their work and lives with us that we cannot thank them individually, but we would not have been able to write about teaching or student learning without their contributions as well.

We also thank the many others whose input and feedback have been essential to making this book what it is now, including imprint editor Cathy Fleischer, the anonymous NCTE reviewers, friends who have read drafts from the earliest stages of our writing process, and the many others who have shared their stories of teaching, learning, and assessing language.

Finally, we would like to acknowledge the National Writing Project and in particular the Area 3 Writing Project, where we both found an enduring community of teachers who care about literacy and the learning of all their students.

NCTE Position Paper on the Role of English Teachers in Educating English Language Learners (ELLs)

Prepared by the NCTE ELL Task Force
Approved by the NCTE Executive Committee, April 2006

This position paper is designed to address the knowledge and skills mainstream teachers need to have in order to develop effective curricula that engage English language learners, develop their academic skills, and help them negotiate their identities as bilingual learners. More specifically, this paper addresses the language and literacy needs of these learners as they participate and learn in English-medium classes. NCTE has made clear bilingual students' right to maintain their native languages (see "On Affirming the CCCC 'Students' Right to Their Own Language'" 2003). Thus, this paper addresses ways teachers can help these students develop English as well as ways they can support their students' bilingualism. In the United States bilingual learners, more commonly referred to as English language learners, are defined as students who know a language other than English and are learning English. Students' abilities range from being non-English speakers to being fully proficient. The recommendations in this paper apply to all of them.

Context

The National Clearinghouse for English Language Acquisition (NCELA) reported that in 2003–04 there were over five million English language learners (ELLs) in schools in the United States (NCELA, 2004). In the last ten years the ELL population has grown 65%, and the diversity of those students continues to challenge teachers and schools. Although 82% of ELLs in the United States are native Spanish speakers, Hopstock and Stephenson (2003) found that school districts identified over 350 different first languages for their second language learners.

Federal, state, and local policies have addressed the education of bilingual learners by implementing different types of programs. Different models of bilingual education, English as a Second Language, English immersion, and integration into mainstream classes, sometimes referred to as submersion, are among the most common approaches. Preferences for the types of programs have changed over time, responding to demographic and political pressures. (For a historical and descriptive summary, see NCTE's "Position Statement on Issues in ESL and Bilingual Education"; Brisk, 2006; Crawford, 2004.)

The best way to educate bilingual learners has been at the center of much controversy. Research points to the advantage of quality bilingual programs (Greene, 1997; Ramirez, 1992; Rolstad, Mahoney, & Glass, 2005; Thomas & Collier, 2002; Willig, 1985) and the benefits of ESL instruction when language is taught through content (Freeman, Y. S., & Freeman, D. E., 1998; Marcia, 2000).

The Role of English Teachers in Educating ELLs

For a variety of reasons, however, the majority of ELLs find themselves in mainstream classrooms taught by teachers with little or no formal professional development in teaching such students (Barron & Menken, 2002; Kindler, 2002). Although improving the education of ELLs has been proposed as a pressing national educational priority (Waxman & Téllez, 2002), many teachers are not adequately prepared to work with a linguistically diverse student population (American Federation of Teachers, 2004; Fillmore & Snow, 2002; Gándara, Rumberger, Maxwell-Jolly, & Callahan, 2003; Menken & Antunez, 2001; Nieto, 2003).

Teachers working to better meet the needs of linguistically diverse students need support. NCTE encourages English teachers to collaborate and work closely with ESL and bilingual teaching professionals, who can offer classroom support, instructional advice, and general insights into second language acquisition. School administrators should support and encourage teachers to attend workshops and professional conferences that regularly offer sessions on bilingual learners, particularly in the areas of reading and writing. Schools should also consider seeking professional development for their teachers from neighboring colleges.

In turn, colleges and universities providing teacher education should offer all preservice teachers, as well as teachers pursuing advanced degree work, preparation in teaching linguistically diverse learners in their future classrooms. Coursework should be offered on second language writing and reading, and on second language acquisition, as well as on culture, and should be encouraged for all teachers.

Who Are the Students?

Bilingual students differ in various ways, including level of oral English proficiency, literacy ability in both the heritage language and English, and cultural backgrounds. English language learners born in the United States often develop conversational language abilities in English but lack academic language proficiency. Newcomers, on the other hand, need to develop both conversational and academic English. Education previous to entering U.S. schools helps determine students' literacy levels in their native language. Some learners may have age-/grade-level skills, while others have limited or no literacy because of the quality of previous schooling, interrupted schooling due to wars or migration, and other circumstances (Suárez-Orozco & Suárez-Orozco, 2001). Given the wide range of English language learners and their backgrounds, it is important that all teachers take the time to learn about their students, particularly in terms of their literacy histories.

Immigrant students and the children of immigrants in the United States come from many cultural backgrounds. The background knowledge English learners bring to school greatly affects their performance. For this reason, teachers of English language learners should be sure to build background for content lessons rather than assuming that bilingual students come with the same background knowledge as mainstream students.

Teaching Bilingual Learners in Mainstream Classrooms

This section specifically addresses teaching language, reading, and writing, as well as the specific kinds of academic literacy that are often a part of most English and language arts curricula. Although English language arts teachers have literacy as the focus of their teaching, many of these suggestions are useful for teachers working in the content areas as well. To acquire academic content through English, English language learners need to learn English. The academic language that students need in the different content areas differs, and students need scaffolding to help them to learn both the English language and the necessary content. For English language learners, teachers need to consider content objectives as well as English language development objectives.

Bilinguals need three types of knowledge to become literate in a second language. They need to know the second language; they need to know literacy; and they need world knowledge (Bernhardt, 1991). The sections below list key ideas for helping English language learners develop academic English proficiency. More detailed information on the topics covered in this section can be obtained from the topical bibliography compiled as part of this project.

To teach bilingual learners, teachers must get to know their learners.

Knowledge of the Students

Knowledge of the students is key to good teaching. Because teachers relate to students both as learners and as children or adolescents, teachers must establish how they will address these two types of relationships, what they need to know about their students, and how they will acquire this knowledge. The teacher-learner relationship implies involvement between teachers and students around subject matter and language and literacy proficiency in both languages. Adult-child relationships are more personal and should include the family. Focusing on both types of relationships bridges the gap between school and the world outside it, a gap that is especially important for many bilingual students whose world differs greatly from school.

Teaching Language

Second language learners need to develop academic proficiency in English to master content-area subjects. Teachers can provide effective instruction for these students by:

- Recognizing that second language acquisition is a gradual developmental process and is built on students' knowledge and skill in their native language;
- Providing authentic opportunities to use language in a nonthreatening environment;
- Teaching key vocabulary connected with the topic of the lesson;
- Teaching academic oral language in the context of various content areas;
- Teaching text- and sentence-level grammar in context to help students understand the structure and style of the English language;
- Teaching the specific features of language students need to communicate in social as well as academic contexts.

The Role of English Teachers in Educating ELLs

Teaching Literacy: Reading

Bilingual students also need to learn to read and write effectively in order to succeed in school.

Teachers can support English language learners' literacy development by:

- Introducing classroom reading materials that are culturally relevant;
- Connecting the readings with the students' background knowledge and experiences;
- Encouraging students to discuss the readings, including the cultural dimensions of the text;
- Having students read a more accessible text on the topic before reading the assigned text;
- Asking families to read with students a version in the heritage language;
- Replacing discrete skill exercises and drills with many opportunities to read;
- Providing opportunities for silent reading in either the students' first language or in English;
- Reading aloud frequently to allow students to become familiar with and appreciate the sounds and structures of written language;
- Reading aloud while students have access to the text to facilitate connecting oral and written modalities;
- Stimulating students' content knowledge of the text before introducing the text;
- Teaching language features, such as text structure, vocabulary, and text- and sentence-level grammar to facilitate comprehension of the text;
- Recognizing that first and second language growth increases with abundant reading and writing.

Support reading comprehension by:

- Relating the topic to the cultural experiences of the students;
- "Front loading" comprehension via a walk through the text or a preview of the main ideas, and other strategies that prepare students for the topic of the text;
- Having students read a more accessible text on the topic before reading the assigned text;
- Asking families to read with students a version in the heritage language;
- Doing pre-reading activities that elicit discussion of the topic;
- Teaching key vocabulary essential for the topic;
- Recognizing that experiences in writing can be used to clarify understanding of reading.

Teaching Literacy: Writing

Writing well in English is often the most difficult skill for English language learners to master. Many English language learners are still acquiring vocabulary and syntactic competence in their writing. Students may show varying degrees of acquisition, and not all second language writers will have the same difficulties or challenges. Teachers should be aware

The Role of English Teachers in Educating ELLs

that English language learners may not be familiar with terminology and routines often associated with writing instruction in the United States, including writing process, drafting, revision, editing, workshop, conference, audience, purpose, or genre. Furthermore, certain elements of discourse, particularly in terms of audience and persuasion, may differ across cultural contexts. The same is true for textual borrowing and plagiarism. The CCCC Statement on Second Language Writing and Writers is a useful resource for all teachers of writing to examine.

Teachers can provide instructional support for English language learners in their writing by:

- Providing a nurturing environment for writing;
- Introducing cooperative, collaborative writing activities which promote discussion;
- Encouraging contributions from all students, and promoting peer interaction to support learning;
- Replacing drills and single-response exercises with time for writing practice;
- Providing frequent meaningful opportunities for students to generate their own texts;
- Designing writing assignments for a variety of audiences, purposes, and genres, and scaffolding the writing instruction;
- Providing models of well-organized papers for the class. Teachers should consider glossing sample papers with comments that point to the specific aspects of the paper that make it well written;
- Offering comments on the strength of the paper, in order to indicate areas where the student is meeting expectations;
- Making comments explicit and clear (both in written response and in oral responses). Teachers should consider beginning feedback with global comments (content and ideas, organization, thesis) and then move on to more local concerns (or mechanical errors) when student writers are more confident with the content of their draft;
- Giving more than one suggestion for change—so that students still maintain control of their writing;
- Not assuming that every learner understands how to cite sources or what plagiarism is. Teachers should consider talking openly about citation and plagiarism in class, exploring the cultural values that are implicit in the rules of plagiarism and textual borrowing, and noting that not all cultures ascribe to the same rules and guidelines. Students should be provided with strategies for avoiding plagiarism.

Teaching Language and Content

The best way to help students learn both English and the knowledge of school subjects is to teach language through content. This should not replace reading and writing instruction in English, nor study of literature and grammar. There are three key reasons to do this:

1. **Students get both language and content.**
   Research has shown that students can learn English and subject matter content material

at the same time. Students don't need to delay the study of science or literature until they reach high levels of English. Instead, they can learn both simultaneously. Given the time limitations older students face, it is crucial that classes provide them with both academic content-area knowledge and academic English.

2. **Language is kept in its natural context.**
When teachers teach science in English, students learn science terms as they study biology or chemistry. The vocabulary occurs naturally as students read and discuss science texts.

3. **Students have reasons to use language for real purposes.**
The primary purpose of school is to help students develop the knowledge of different academic disciplines. When academic content is presented in English, students focus on the main purpose of schooling: learning science, math, social studies, or literature. In the process, they also learn English.

Selecting Materials

- Choose a variety of texts around a theme.
- Choose texts at different levels of difficulty.
- Choose reading and writing materials that represent the cultures of the students in the class.
- When possible, include texts in the native languages of the ELLs in the class. The following considerations should be used as a guide for choosing texts that support bilingual learners:
  - Materials should include both literature and informational texts.
  - Materials should include culturally relevant texts.
  - Authentic materials should be written to inform or entertain, not to teach a grammar point or a letter-sound correspondence.
  - The language of the text should be natural.
  - If translated, the translation should be good language.
  - Materials should include predictable text for emergent readers.
  - Materials should include texts with nonlinguistic cues that support comprehension (For a more comprehensive checklist, see Freeman, Y. S., & Freeman, D. E., 2002; Freeman, D. E., & Freeman, Y. S., 2004).

Low-Level Literacy Immigrant Students

Late-arrival immigrant and refugee students with low literacy skills have been found to benefit from Newcomer programs or Welcome Centers designed for 1-3 semesters of high school (Boyson & Short, 2003; Schnur, 1999; Short, 2002). The focus is to help students acquire beginning English skills and guide students' acculturation to the U.S. school system before enrollment in regular ESL language support programs or content-area classrooms. The integration of such programs in high school English departments should be encouraged.

Conclusion

As the number of bilingual learners in mainstream classes increases, it becomes even more important for mainstream teachers to use effective practices to engage these students so that they can acquire the academic English and the content-area knowledge they need for school success. The guidelines offered here are designed as initial suggestions for teachers to follow. However, we recognize that all teachers need much more. Teachers need continued support and professional development to enable all their students, including their bilingual students, to succeed.

References

American Federation of Teachers. (March, 2004). *Closing the achievement gap: Focus on Latino students* (Policy Brief 17). Retrieved March 28, 2006, from http://www.aft.org/teachers/pusbs-reports/index.htm#english.

Barron, V., & Menken, K. (2002). *What are the characteristics of the bilingual education and ESL teacher shortage?* Washington, D.C.: National Clearinghouse for English Language Acquisition and Language Instruction Educational Programs.

Bernhardt, E. B. (1991). A psycholinguistic perspective on second language literacy. Reading in Two Languages. *AILA Review, 8*, 31–44.

Boyson, B. A., & Short, D. J. (2003). *Secondary school newcomer programs in the United States* (Research Report 12). Santa Cruz, CA, and Washington, DC: Center for Research on Education Diversity & Excellence.

Brisk, M. E. (2006). *Bilingual education: From compensatory to quality schooling.* (2nd ed.) Mahwah, NJ: Erlbaum.

Crawford, J. (2004). *Educating English learners.* Los Angeles: Bilingual Education Services.

De Jong, E. J. (2002). Effective bilingual education: From theory to academic achievement in a two-way bilingual program. *Bilingual Research Journal, 26*(1), 1–15.

Fillmore, L. W., & Snow, C. (2002). What teachers need to know about language. In C. T. Adger, C. Snow, & D. Christian (Eds.), *What teachers need to know about language* (pp. 7–53). Washington, DC: Center for Applied Linguistics.

Freeman, D. E., and Freeman, Y. S. (2004). *Essential linguistics: What you need to know to teach reading, ESL, spelling, phonics, and grammar.* Portsmouth, NH: Heinemann.

Freeman, Y. S., & Freeman, D. E. (1998). *ESL/EFL teaching: Principles for success.* Portsmouth, NH: Heinemann.

Freeman, Y. S., and Freeman, D. E. (2002). *Closing the achievement gap.* Portsmouth, NH: Heinemann.

Gándara, P., Rumberger, R., Maxwell-Jolly, J., & Callahan, R. (2003). English learners in California schools: Unequal resources, unequal outcomes. *Education Policy Analysis Archives, 11*(36). Retrieved March 28, 2006, from http://epaa.asu.edu/.

Gibbons, P. (2002). *Scaffolding language, scaffolding learning: Teaching second language learners in the mainstream classroom.* Portsmouth, NH: Heinemann.

Greene, J. P. (1997). A meta-analysis of the Rossell and Baker review of bilingual education research. *Bilingual Research Journal, 21*.

The Role of English Teachers in Educating ELLs

Hopstock, P. & Stephenson, T. (2003). *Native languages of limited English proficient students.* U.S. Department of Education. Retrieved March 5, 2006.

Kindler, A. L. (2002). *Survey of the states' limited English proficient students and available educational programs and services 1999-2000 summary report.* Washington, DC: National Clearinghouse for English Language Acquisition and Language Instruction Education Programs (NCELA). Retrieved Dec. 26, 2003, from http://www.ncela.gwu.edu.

Krashen, S. (1996). *Under attack: The case against bilingual education.* Culver City, CA: Language Education Associates.

McQuillan, J., & Tse, L. (1997). Does research matter? An analysis of media opinion of bilingual education, 1984–1994. *Bilingual Research Journal, 20*(1), 1–27.

Menken, K., & Antunez, B. (2001). *An overview of the preparation and certification of teachers working with limited English proficient students.* Washington, DC: National Clearinghouse of Bilingual Education. Retrieved July 28, 2003, from http://www.ericsp.org/pages/digests/ncbe.pdf.

NCELA. (2006). *The growing number of limited English proficient students 1991–2002.* Washington, DC: U.S. Department of Education.

Nieto, S. M. (2003). *What keeps teachers going?* New York: Teachers College.

Pally, M. (Ed.) (2000). *Sustained content teaching in academic ESL/EFL: A practical approach.* Boston: Houghton Mifflin.

Ramirez, J. D. (1992). Executive summary. *Bilingual Research Journal, 16*, 1–62.

Rolstad, K., Mahoney, K., & Glass, G. V. (2005). The big picture: A meta-analysis of program effectiveness research on English language learners. *Educational Policy, 19*, 572–594.

Schnur, B. (1999). A newcomer's high school. *Educational Leadership, 56*(7), 50–52.

Short, D. J. (2002). Newcomer programs: An educational alternative for secondary immigrant students. *Education and Urban Society, 34*(2), 173–198.

Solomon, J., & Rhodes, N. (1995). *Conceptualizing academic language.* Washington, DC: The National Center for Research on Cultural Diversity and Second Language Learning.

Suárez-Orozco, C., & Suárez-Orozco, M. M. (2001). *Children of immigration.* Cambridge, MA: Harvard University.

Thomas, W. P., & Collier, V. P. (2002). *A national study of school effectiveness for language minority students' long-term academic achievement.* Santa Cruz, CA: Center for Research on Education, Diversity & Excellence, University of California, Santa Cruz.

Waxman, H. C., & Téllez, K. (2002). *Research synthesis on effective teaching practices for English language learners* (Publication Series No. 3). Philadelphia: Mid-Atlantic Regional Educational Laboratory.

Willig, A. C. (1985). A meta-analysis of selected studies on the effectiveness of bilingual education. *Review of Educational Research, 55*(3), 269–317.

For more resources to support English language learners, see http://www.ncte.org/positions/statements/teacherseducatingell.

Statement of Terminology and Glossary

Steven Alvarez, St. John's University

Betsy Gilliland, University of Hawai'i Mānoa

Christina Ortmeier-Hooper, University of New Hampshire

Melinda J. McBee Orzulak, Bradley University

Shannon Pella, California State University, Sacramento

As authors of the various books in the Teaching English Language Learners strand of the NCTE Principles in Practice (PIP) imprint, we have made a concerted effort to use consistent terminology in these volumes. All of us have thought long and hard about the ways in which we label and describe bilingual and ELL students and the programs that often provide these students with additional support. Even so, readers will notice some variation in terms used to describe students, classrooms, and teaching practices. The concern over terminology is part of a long-standing discussion and trends in the labeling of these students, as well as of the fields that conduct research on teachers and students working across languages to teach and learn English. Often the shifting among terms leads to confusion and contention for teachers, administrators, teacher educators, and policymakers.

To address this confusion and tension, we begin each book in this strand with a glossary of common terms and acronyms that are part of current discussions about meeting the needs of these students in English language arts classrooms and beyond. For many readers, the terms themselves and the ongoing shift to new terms can be alienating, the jargon dividing readers into insiders and outsiders. But often the shift in terms has a great deal to do with both policy and issues of identity for students. For example, up until the No Child Left Behind (NCLB) Act of 2001, most educational documents referred to these students as *bilingual* or *ESL*, both of which acknowledge that English is a second language and that a student has a first language as well.

The term *English language learner* was adopted with NCLB and brought into our schools and the larger public discourse. In fact, in 2002 the US Department of Education renamed the Office of Bilingual Education and Minority Languages Affairs. It became the Office of English Language Acquisition, Language Enhancement and Academic Achievement for Limited English Proficient Students, now identified simply as the Office of English Language Acquisition (OELA). The change indicated a shift away from acknowledging students' home languages or bilingual abilities. Close to two decades later, the term *English language learner* remains prominent in educational policy and in many textbooks geared toward teachers and teacher educators. Its prominence and familiarity in the literature makes it an accessible way to talk about these students. Yet, as we have heard from many students through the years, the term *English language learner* can also be limiting. As one student asked, "When do I stop being an English language learner and get to just be an English language user?" The term also works against efforts to acknowledge the competencies and linguistically sophisticated talents these students have as translators, bilingual speakers, and cross-cultural negotiators.

Statement of Terminology and Glossary

In these PIP volumes, we use the term *English language learner* as a way to reach out to readers who see and hear this term regularly used in their schools, in their hallways, and in other helpful books in the field. However, some of us also use the terms *multilingual* or *bilingual* in order to encourage a discussion of these young people not simply as novice English learners but as individuals with linguistic and academic competencies they have gained from bilingual/multilingual experiences and literacies.

Glossary

Bilingual, multilingual, or plurilingual: These terms refer to the ability to use (i.e., speak, write, and/or read) multiple languages. For many ELL-designated students in US schools, English is actually the third or fourth language they have learned, making *bilingual* not necessarily an accurate term.

Emergent bilingual: This term has been proposed as a more appropriate term than *LEP* or *ELL*, because it points to possibilities of developing bilingualism rather than focusing on language limits or deficiencies (García, 2009).

English as a foreign language (EFL): Refers to non-native English-speaking students who are learning English in a country where English is not the primary language.

English as an international language (EIL) or English as a lingua franca (ELF): These are terms used to refer to global conceptions of English, or English used for communication between members of various nations.

English as a second language (ESL): Readers may be most familiar with this term because it has been used as an overarching term for students, programs, and/or a field of study. Currently the term usually refers to programs of instruction (i.e., study of English in an English-speaking country); however, *ESL* was used in the past to refer to English language learning students.

English language learner (ELL): In keeping with the terminology used in the *NCTE Position Paper on the Role of English Teachers in Educating English Language Learners (ELLs)*, this PIP strand employs the term *ELL*, which is commonly used in secondary schools as the short form of *English language learner*. The term refers to a complex, heterogeneous range of students who are in the process of learning English.

English learner (EL): This is the preferred term of the California Department of Education (and, increasingly, other states). California is the state with the largest number and percentage of emergent bilingual students enrolled in public schools. Over the past twenty years, California has moved from *LEP* to *ELL* and, most recently, from *ELL* to *EL*.

First language (L1) and second language (L2): *L1* has been used to refer to students' "mother tongue" or "home language" as they learn additional languages (referred to as *L2*).

Generation 1.5: This term, originally used in higher education, often refers to students who have been long-term residents in the United States but who were born abroad (al-

Statement of Terminology and Glossary

though the term is sometimes also used to refer to US-born children of recent immigrants). The designation of 1.5 describes their feelings of being culturally between first- and second-generation immigrants; they are often fluent in spoken English but may still be working to command aspects of written English, especially academic writing. As long-term residents, these students may reject *ESL* as a term that has been used to refer to recent immigrants to the United States.

Limited English proficiency (LEP): This abbreviation may be used in some educational contexts to refer to a designation used by the US Department of Education. Many scholars see this as a deficit term because of its focus on subtractive language (language that implies a deficiency) under a monolingual assumption of proficiency.

Long-term English language learner (LTELL): Currently in use in some states, this term refers to K–12 students who have been enrolled in US schools for many years and continue to be stuck with the ELL designation long past the time it should take for redesignation. Like Generation 1.5 students, LTELLs may have spent most if not all of their education in US schools. For a variety of reasons, including family mobility, inconsistent educational programs, and personal reasons, they have not had opportunities to learn academic language sufficiently to pass English language proficiency tests and other measures of proficiency for redesignation (Olsen, 2010).

Mainstream: This term is increasingly antiquated due to shifting demographics in the United States. In practice, it often refers to nonremedial, nonhonors, nonsheltered classes and programs. Sometimes it is used to refer to native or monolingual English speakers as a norm; changing demographics, however, mean that schools increasingly have a majority of culturally and linguistically diverse students, so it's been argued that a linguistically diverse classroom is the "New Mainstream" (Enright, 2011).

Monolingual: This term is used to refer to people who speak only one language, although often this label masks speakers' fluent use of multiple dialects, or variations, of English—an issue of particular concern when working with culturally diverse students who use other varieties of English (such as Hawai'i Pidgin or African American Vernacular) in their lives outside of school. The monolingual English label can mask these diverse students' need to learn academic English just as much as their immigrant classmates do. Much of what this PIP strand discusses is relevant to students who utilize multiple varieties of English; teachers can support these students by acknowledging their multilingualism and helping them learn to use English for academic and other purposes.

Native or non-native English speakers (NES, NNES): Some materials contrast native English speakers (NES) with non-native English speakers (NNES). As with *monolingual*, the term *native speaker* is increasingly unclear, given how many long-term ELLs speak English fluently without a "foreign" accent and yet technically have another world language as their home or first language.

Newcomer: Some school districts have separate one-year programs for "newcomers," or students who are newly arrived in the United States, in which students learn not just "surviv-

Statement of Terminology and Glossary

al" English, but also how school works in the United States. As the position statement discusses, it's sometimes argued that newcomer programs benefit "low-level literacy immigrant students" and/or students with interrupted formal education who may have limited literacy in their first language (L1). Other newcomers may be fully literate in L1, especially by high school, and may or may not benefit from being isolated from the mainstream curriculum. For older students, the challenge is to move away from "low-level" ideas of literacy assessment that may discount the literacies of these students.

Resident or local bilingual, multilingual, or plurilingual: These terms are sometimes used to refer to students who reside in the United States (in contrast to those who are on student visas). Resident students may or may not be US citizens, others may not have permanent resident status, while still others may not have immigration documentation at all.

References

Enright, K. A. (2011). Language and literacy for a new mainstream. *American Educational Research Journal, 48*(1), 80–118. doi: 10.3102/0002831210368989

García, O. (2009). Emergent bilinguals and TESOL: What's in a name? *TESOL Quarterly, 43*(2), 322–26. doi:10.1002/j.1545-7249.2009.tb00172.x

Olsen, L. (2010). *Reparable harm: Fulfilling the unkept promise of educational opportunity for California's long term English learners.* Long Beach, CA: Californians Together.

Accountability for Equity

So They May Learn and Thrive: Accountability for Equity

Consider these two scenarios:

> Seventeen-year-old Manuel[1] is not doing well in school. He frequently
> dozes off when he should be reading silently from his textbook. When
> he turns in written assignments, instead of providing critical analysis
> of readings in the textbook, he just copies lines from the passages. His
> longer essays often contain sentences that are so garbled the main
> idea is completely missing. Manuel has attended school in the district
> since third grade, and even though he speaks fluently with teachers
> and peers, he is still classified as an English language learner. His
> English teacher, Renata McKay, dreads the year-end standardized
> tests because she is certain Manuel will either randomly fill in bubbles
> on the answer sheet or leave entire sections blank. At Roosevelt High
> School, Manuel's test scores will not only determine whether he is
> allowed to graduate next year, but they will also be used to evaluate
> Renata's teaching effectiveness.

At Chavez High School, fifteen-year-old Janice is doing well in school. After living in the United States for three years, she is classified as an "advanced English language learner" and is on track to be reclassified as "English fluent" within the next year. She loves to read young adult novels, especially when she can discuss the plot and characters with her three classmates who are also reading the same book. Although she freely admits that she is still learning English, she uses strategies she has learned from her teacher, Vik Singh, to analyze unfamiliar words and sentences and figure out what they mean. Janice regularly writes short texts about the books she has read and collaborates with classmates to analyze published texts and write essays that Vik displays on a bulletin board outside the classroom door. Every quarter, he invites the principal, the students' parents, and other community members to stop by the classroom to read what his students have written. Although Janice's standardized test scores are not fully reflective of what she has learned to do in class, these visitors can see that she is learning and that Vik is indeed an effective teacher.

These two hypothetical scenarios, reflective of many classrooms where we have taught and observed, raise essential questions in this age of accountability: What kind of accountability measures truly demonstrate multilingual[2] students' learning? How do these measures reflect the planning and teaching that teachers do to help their students grow? Renata's school administrators treat a single standardized test as all the evidence they need of both the students' learning and the teacher's effectiveness. Vik's school, on the other hand, recognizes the limited information that one test can provide.

These accountability issues concern all of us—but become particularly challenging for mainstream English language arts (ELA) teachers who may have a handful of multilingual speakers in their classrooms. Concerned about accountability for *all*, these teachers may wrestle with finding the best ways to help students who already struggle with English.

We are teachers and teacher educators who believe deeply that language diversity is an asset and a valuable resource. As such, we are committed to supporting and developing the multilingualism of the students in our classrooms and the language pedagogies of our colleagues. Having worked with both mainstream and English language learner (ELL)-specialist teachers in diverse schools and universities for the past twenty years, we have seen how national and state-level accountability policies have changed and how teachers and students have been caught in the crosshairs. Though we doubt that policymakers intended to punish teachers for working with struggling students, we have seen how inappropriate tests have been used to make claims about students' knowledge and teachers' ability to teach. In terms of equity, we feel that these uses of assessment practices are unfair to both the students, who do not have the language to access the content or demonstrate what they know, and the teachers, who are judged for their students' performance on tests that do not validly show what students have learned. In this book, we propose an approach that helps increase equitable access to the academic language and challenging content of assessment for multilingual learners.

> Look at the rosters of your current or most recent classes. Which of these students are classified as ELLs? Which have been reclassified since enrolling in your school or district? Which students speak multiple languages in and out of school? How do you know?

We are writing this book as a companion to the *NCTE Position Paper on the Role of English Teachers in Educating English Language Learners* (which going forward we will refer to as the ELL Brief). The book addresses accountability issues related to many of the sections covered in the ELL Brief, including "Knowledge of the Students," "Teaching Language," "Teaching Literacy: Reading," "Teaching Literacy: Writing," "Teaching Language and Content," and "Selecting Materials." The principles listed in each of these sections of the brief offer starting points for teachers as they plan for and teach literacy to their multilingual students within an institutional environment that is overwhelmingly focused on narrowly defined notions of accountability. One gap in the position paper, however, is consideration of how teachers in mainstream classrooms can evaluate language and literacy learning in ways that both support these students' growth and prepare them for the high-stakes tests that may affect their own, their teachers', and their schools' futures. This book intends to fill that gap, making connections between the ELL Brief's teaching recommendations and teachers' accountability concerns.

Our goal with this book is to help mainstream ELA teachers and other teachers working with diverse groups of learners find ways to help their multilingual students succeed—and to represent their learning through a variety of assessments: formative, summative, and standardized. We have found that when ELA teachers modify some of their curricular approaches by bringing in a greater emphasis on academic language, all students (fluent English speakers and multilingual learners alike) benefit. In the pages that follow, then, we describe how one approach familiar to most ELA teachers, genre-based instruction (GBI), can be amplified using the tools of systemic functional linguistics (SFL) that may be familiar to ELL teachers. Connecting these two approaches can create a comprehensive instructional program that supports ELLs in learning grade-level content and the academic language they need to access that content and demonstrate their learning on formative and summative assessments. We also illustrate how GBI and SFL further help teachers to support multilingual students in learning how to take standardized

Multilingual Student Profile

Azra

Although she is technically a senior, eighteen-year-old Azra is planning to stay in school for another year in order to take classes she needs for graduation and college preparation. She immigrated with her parents and older brother to California from Pakistan two years ago and started high school in the Newcomers English Language Development (ELD) class. Her teachers rapidly promoted her through the levels so that now she is in the highest level ELD class and will take a mainstream English class next year. Azra wears hijab, a traditional Muslim headscarf, with jeans and a T-shirt underneath. She enjoys reading novels written in Urdu and shares favorite quotations with her friends on Facebook. She writes poetry in Urdu with her sister. In Pakistan, her middle school teacher made a strong impression on her understanding of how to write for academic purposes: "She talks a lot about writing, like she said don't just memorize things, first read them and understand them; if you don't understand then ask me; if you don't understand, you can ask me whatever you want. Then you can write it in your own words." Azra has been studying English since second grade, learning vocabulary and reading short stories. During her advanced ELD class, she usually spends her class time working on the assignments and frequently finishes well before the end of the period. If she has assignments for her other classes, she will then proceed to pull out a US history or geometry textbook and do her homework. She plans to spend her summer break reading books.

tests without having to resort to mindless "teaching to the test," another common problem that recent accountability measures have engendered.

To bring these ideas to life, we present stories of teachers who have used these tools to modify their instruction in ways that any teacher can incorporate into day-to-day teaching. We do not want you to feel like you need to create completely separate lessons or assessments for your multilingual learners, nor that you need to study for an entirely new credential in order to make language and content accessible to language learners. Instead, we want to show how teachers with little additional training beyond their English language arts credentials were able to identify the core language structures students would need to know within standards-based literacy lessons (reading and/or writing) and to design learning experiences that both taught the language and content and allowed them to assess how well their multilingual students had learned the language and content.

Accountability as a concept is a good thing. A functioning society depends on holding people accountable for their behavior and actions. The past decades have shown what happens when some of the largest and most trusted institutions—financial, government, and corporate—have weakly enforced accountability systems. We have seen scandal, corruption, and mismanagement as a result of lax accountability. Accountability can prevent problems and be proactive through holding institutions responsible for their labor, environmental, and civil rights practices. Unfortunately, accountability can also be misappropriated. Schools, for example, are institutions within which accountability systems are necessary, and yet these systems have often caused more damage than good.

Why is this so? Accountability in preK–12 education is too often limited to externally designed and scored assessments that result in externally determined rewards and consequences. These measures, as any teacher can tell you, represent a snapshot, and often not a very good one, of what students are able to do at a single moment in time. Most state-mandated assessments measure standards-based proficiency instead of measuring growth toward proficiency, thereby painting an incomplete picture of both students' skill levels and teachers' efficacy. Annual state tests rarely (if ever) capture students' full range of knowledge, and as we stress in this book, they have been shown repeatedly not to illustrate fairly what culturally and linguistically diverse students know and can do. As accountability tools, externally designed and scored assessments are not responsive to the people at the heart of schools: the students— and in particular, linguistically diverse students. We wrote this book to reimagine accountability by exploring ways that we as teachers can hold *ourselves* accountable for teaching and assessing our students' learning. We focus in particular on mainstream teachers' accountability for the language and literacy development of English language learners and other multilingual students, a growing population of students with significant linguistic and cultural assets.

We view accountability as a positive, internal, and classroom contextualized process, a way to learn about our practices and the impact of our practices on our students' learning. We believe that when we hold *ourselves* accountable for assessing our students' growth, and focus on our own professional learning as a result, accountability is no longer something that is done *to* us but is instead in our locus of control. We see accountability as a key factor in promoting equitable educational opportunities for *all* students, but especially for the English language learners in our classrooms and our schools.

Our central argument in this book is that authentic, formative assessments are important for accountability and that assessment and instruction are interdependent. Classroom teachers as well as site-based support staff play an essential role in assessing the academic progress of English language learners, and we believe that teachers can make realistic, feasible shifts in their instructional practices to support

Definitions

Accountability in teaching multilingual learners means taking responsibility for helping students learn what they need to know (content and language) for success in school and life.

Assessment means identifying all students' strengths and learning needs across the academic year. Formative assessment happens throughout every unit as you check informally on how well students understand the learning objectives and then adjust your instruction to ensure that all students have access to course content and academic language and skills. Summative assessment occurs at the end of a unit or term when you check to see how much of the objectives students have learned.

Equity means ensuring that *all* students have access to challenging grade-level content, academic language, and literacy skills, as well as providing appropriate assessments that allow *all* students to demonstrate their growth, knowledge, and skills.

multilingual students' learning. Thus, in addition to externally designed and scored assessments, accountability is located in teachers' daily instructional and ongoing formative assessment practices, both of which develop the assets and serve the needs of the students in our classrooms. With careful attention to curriculum planning, all teachers can support, guide, assess, and document their students' growth through well-designed learning experiences and ongoing formative assessment.

We hope that as teachers, we can see ourselves as the primary agents of accountability, and as a result, we will feel empowered to avoid the external pressures that often drive teaching in the wrong direction for English language learners. Accountability for equity means supporting multilingual students as they access challenging and relevant grade-level content and demonstrate their knowledge in meaningful ways.

What Is Accountability?

Merriam-Webster's online dictionary defines *accountability* as "an obligation or willingness to accept responsibility or to account for one's actions." This definition fits well with what we advocate in this book. Although accountability in the preK–12 education of English language learners is typically measured though externally designed assessment scores, teachers should also play a leading role.

What does this definition of accountability mean for teachers of English language learners? We argue along with researchers Alison Bailey and Patricia Carroll (2015) that in addition to externally designed and scored formal tests, all teachers play a major role in assessing the literacy and language development of English language learners. Because assessment and instruction are inextricably linked, being accountable for teaching English language learners includes providing a variety of language supports, academically challenging critical thinking experiences, and ongoing formative assessment; these types of iterative assessments not only improve teaching and learning opportunities for students but also propel teachers toward continued professional development. We think of accountability as arising out of these multiple experiences: it is located in a teacher's continuous cycle of well-designed, responsive instruction and ongoing formative assessment, which includes observations of students' interactions with their classmates and participation in class, interviews and conferences with students about course concepts, and "moment-to-moment . . . contingent instructional responses to students' immediate learning needs" (Bailey & Carroll, 2015, p. 268). Through ongoing formative assessment, teachers can respond quickly to provide students with feedback at the moment they need support. Furthermore, ongoing formative assessment allows teachers to notice areas where ELL students need individualized language or content support in ways that are different from the needs of the fluent English speakers in the class. Such practices, accompanied by other curricular and professional support, have been shown to improve ELL students' performance on formal assessments (Goldenberg & Coleman, 2010).

Thus, we situate accountability in the real practices of classroom teachers as they engage in an iterative process of identifying language demands, articulating language objectives, designing language supports for critical thinking, and engaging in the ongoing formative assessment of English learners. These processes provide information for improved teaching practices and a window into teachers' own professional development needs.

Accountability for What?

For what are teachers to be held accountable? In one sense, we should be accountable *to our schools* by supporting our students to perform to the best of their abilities on standardized tests and to demonstrate their ability to meet standards-based expectations for their grade level. In another—and we believe more important—sense, we are accountable *to our students*, which means making it possible for students to thrive socially, emotionally, and academically by developing language skills, content knowledge, and learning in a variety of areas that may not be evidenced from one isolated test-taking experience. The overreliance on standardized test scores has been widely criticized in more than a decade of research. While we do address preparing multilingual students for high-stakes standardized assessments (in Chapter 6), we suggest that to truly engage and prepare linguistically diverse students for the future, we must focus less on external measures of accountability and more on internal accountability processes through our own teaching and ongoing formative assessment practices.

As classroom teachers, we know that tests can tell us some important things about our students, but research has also documented how school districts with high percentages of immigrant multilingual students have been pressured to "teach to the test" (Jones, Jones, & Hargrove, 2003; Plank & Condliffe, 2013) even as other studies have shown that state standardized tests are often invalid for ELLs (Abedi & Gándara, 2006; Menken, 2010). Research on the impact of high-stakes testing suggests that an overemphasis on teaching to the test in schools with struggling students and multilingual learners leads to test-prep skill drills rather than lifelong literacy learning.

Teaching to the test can be especially harmful to multilingual students. A review of research on high-stakes assessments given during the No Child Left Behind (NCLB) era found that few tests were normed or validated for use with ELLs (Solórzano, 2008). What this means is that in many cases, the complex language used on tests prevents students from understanding what they are supposed to

Multilingual Student Profile

Onasis

Fifteen-year-old Onasis has dark hair gelled into haphazard spikes. He speaks English with a strong Spanish accent, but his ninth-grade teachers don't know that he was actually born in Los Angeles. He began school in California, first learning to read and write in English. Then, when he was in third grade, his parents moved to Mexico and he had to take up reading and writing in Spanish. His family returned to California when he was in eighth grade. He says it is easy to read and write in both languages, although he prefers writing in English. He reads books and magazines in English regularly every week. He also maintains an account on a Mexican social network, where he posts messages to his friends from elementary school. He is studying guitar and hopes to study rumba flamenca in Spain after high school in order to become a professional musician. In class, Onasis participates actively in both the official and unofficial conversations, frequently asking the teachers questions and also rotating in his seat to talk in Spanish with the other boys. He works diligently and wants to understand everything he is reading. When choosing topics for writing, he opts for challenges in order to impress the teachers rather than taking the easy choice. He recognizes, however, that his teachers may not be aware of how much English he actually knows: "I know a lot of English, but my accent's not good. That's why I started from the first, second level." A strategic student, he makes use of his high school's Learning Center, visiting the tutors for help two or three times a week.

do or from showing their knowledge of the content (Abedi, 2010; Abedi & Gándara, 2006). Problems also arise when tests are written with assumptions of students' cultural knowledge. Multilingual students often do not have an equal opportunity to learn the content through high-quality resources or from well-prepared teachers. These problems are multiplied when the test scores are used for purposes beyond those originally intended—such as placement into academic tracks and grade-level retention. While multilingual students may not score well on standardized tests, other assessments (such as portfolios or first language testing) show that they have knowledge and skills that are not revealed through the tests (Solórzano, 2008). Clearly, a single test cannot capture the wide range of multilingual students' abilities and assets.

Multilingual students' preparation for high-stakes assessments and the achievement gap between their performance and that of other students remain of high concern for teachers, schools, and states. State standards have been common since the 1990s, when federal policy (in response to renewed concern about the declining quality of American education) prioritized states' voluntary setting of academic content and performance standards (Goals 2000: Educate America Act, 1994). The 2001 No Child Left Behind legislation highlighted state standards, making them a pillar of the act's emphasis on the federal government's role in monitoring education. As you have likely experienced, NCLB added additional mandates that states create assessments to determine students' progress toward the standards and disaggregate their test score data, reporting scores from subgroups of students, including various ethnic groups, special education students, and English language learners. These regulations were intended to bring greater fairness to students who previously had not received a challenging curriculum; because they were to be tested with the same assessments as native English speakers, their schools would have to teach English learners to the same standards (Shaul & Ganson, 2005). An unintended but powerful outcome of the testing requirement, however, was that schools with high percentages of multilingual students wound up teaching to the test, focusing on rote memorization of facts rather than deeper understanding of concepts.

Just as the numbers of multilingual students in classrooms across the United States are increasing, new standards and assessment policies at the national and state levels are placing even greater importance on the success of these students in school. The Common Core State Standards (CCSS) introduced new tests and new standards that offer little guidance to teachers working with multilingual learners (TESOL, 2013; Valdés, Kibler, & Walqui, 2014). The CCSS were conceived as a remedy to the widely differing requirements of the earlier state standards, which did not allow comparison across states and often did not present a coherent learning trajectory across grade levels. In the English language arts, the CCSS present three overarching shifts from earlier standards with respect to how literacy and academic language are conceptualized:

- Regular practice with complex text and academic language;
- Reading, writing and speaking grounded in evidence from text, both literary and informational; and
- Building knowledge through content-rich nonfiction. (Student Achievement Partners, 2015)

These shifts mean that teaching in general is undergoing a conceptual reframing to focus more deeply on literacy and language over surface-level information.

The latest reauthorization of the federal Elementary and Secondary Education Act, the 2015 Every Student Succeeds Act, takes a few steps back from the centralized concerns of No Child Left Behind but nevertheless continues to pressure teachers of English language learners to prepare their students for high-stakes tests. The new law, which goes into effect for the 2017–18 academic year, still requires annual testing to evaluate student progress toward high academic standards, but it allows states greater flexibility both in which challenging standards they choose (Common Core is one option) and in how they measure accountability, barring a complete reliance on standardized test scores. State goals must include "proficiency on tests, English-language proficiency, and graduation rates" (Klein, 2015, "Goals" para. 2). ELLs' test scores must be reported separately from those of other subgroups and are fully counted alongside their English-fluent peers after only two years in US schools, ignoring research showing that ELL students' content knowledge cannot be distinguished from their English language proficiency until they have achieved academic language proficiency (Carnock, 2015). Although there will be additional developments as the new policy comes into effect, teachers of ELLs remain concerned that they must not only teach their students academic and social English, but also prepare them for further tests and new standards and curriculum.

These changes are especially challenging to implement for teachers of multilingual learners, as one significant gap in the CCSS is a lack of information about how the new standards relate to the education of students who are still learning English. Without any defined specifics for standards or pedagogy, individual states are expected to create or revise their English language proficiency development standards to address English language learner needs. These standards are important because they establish expectations for students' progress through school and the forms and levels of English they learn (Valdés et al., 2014). While the CCSS consortium provides a short resource guide for teachers on its website, the standards provide no clear connections to individual grade-level standards and leave pedagogical and content decisions to individual teachers, which means that it is now more important than ever for teachers to feel comfortable differentiating their instruction to address the varied learning needs of their multilingual students.

If you are a classroom teacher concerned about how best to ensure the success of all your students, including your multilingual learners, these changes may require substantial adaptations to both curriculum and instruction. Our argument in this book, though, is this: teachers who approach accountability as an internal, classroom contextualized process of teaching and formative assessment can help their ELL students survive and thrive. In the coming chapters, we illustrate how teachers hold themselves accountable for assessing learning by supporting their multilingual students to think critically about texts and communicate their thinking verbally, in writing, and across modalities through a variety of language types including academic English.

Accountability to Whom?

Of all of the stakeholders to whom the education system is accountable, including the public (taxpayers and local residents); federal, state, and local governments; school leadership; students; and the families of students and their communities, we focus primarily on teachers' accountability *to students* (see Table 1.1). Holding ourselves accountable to our students means providing them with equitable access to challenging curricula and thoughtful literacy practices, maintaining their linguistic diversity, and supporting students in reaching their future goals.

As teachers are well aware, however, school districts too often lose sight of this notion of accountability to students and focus instead on accountability to outsiders. The external pressures that this kind of accountability creates can lead to a primary focus on the test performances of students who traditionally score at

Table 1.1. Ways to Be Accountable to Stakeholders

Accountability to whom?	Demonstrated through . . .	Where addressed in this book
Students	• Valuing language diversity as an asset and resource • Focusing on real-world literacy • Preparing for college and career • Focusing on genres of school and life • Engaging with culturally diverse and respectful texts	Chapters 3, 4, & 5
	• Teaching how to take tests (show what they already know)	Chapter 6
School (teachers and administrators)	• Preparing ELLs for literacy in subject areas	Chapters 3, 4, & 5
	• Identifying and addressing language demands, setting language objectives, and providing relevant and targeted language supports • Developing shared metalanguage for talking about language within genres across subject areas and grade levels	Chapters 2, 3, 4, & 5
	• Discussing ELL students' test results and planning scaffolds and accommodations • Demonstrating ELL students' learning through alternative assessment forms	Chapter 7
District and state	• Test scores • Other formal assessments • College and career readiness	Chapter 6
Community (and parents)	• Showing language and content knowledge growth • Showing that ELLs can do more than take tests • Emphasizing progress and growth • Bringing families in to learn about assessment policy and how to support students	Chapter 7

the lower end of standardized measures, a focus that can backfire for students who want to learn and teachers who want to help them. Because low-scoring schools tend to have higher proportions of ethnic and linguistic minority students, school-level accountability measures affect these students at greater levels as well (Jones et al., 2003). To raise test scores, schools may refocus the curriculum to better prepare students for taking high-stakes tests (Hillocks, 2002; Menken, 2006, 2008). Since the tests usually measure discrete, basic skills, instruction often focuses on those same skills, ignoring higher-order critical thinking that does not appear on the tests (Anson, 2008; Applebee & Langer, 2009; Hillocks, 2003; Jones et al., 2003).

We want to avoid such situations by designing rich learning experiences that promote language development and content knowledge within the expectations of the mainstream curriculum, as well as build community and interpersonal social skills among students. Additionally, we can supplement information from standardized test scores with well-documented information about our students' growth and learning from classroom-contextualized formative assessment. The scenarios we present in this book, illustrating actual classroom practice, take into account the external systems to which teachers are held accountable: parents, principals, district policies, and others. However, the teachers we describe are focused on holding themselves accountable *to their students*, particularly their English language learners.

Accountability How?

Accountability is measured in multiple ways. Some external accountability systems use data from policy-mandated standardized tests (yearly tests, English language proficiency tests, and high school exit exams) and statistics (graduation and promotion rates, college-going rates, and adequate yearly progress). Accountability is also addressed through fulfillment of curricular requirements (district pacing guides and benchmark assignments). Other measures to hold schools accountable include student and parent satisfaction surveys.

> How many forms of assessment (including tests) are you required to administer in a given academic year? Which are mandated by the state? By the district? Which have high stakes for your students? For you? For your school? What do you and your school site colleagues do with the data from these tests?

Formal tests of standards mastery continue to be a focus under the 2015 reauthorization of the Elementary and Secondary Education Act (Every Student Succeeds), and, as with NCLB, students designated as English language learners must take those tests for school and state accountability purposes.

Two consortia, the Smarter Balanced Assessment Consortium (SBAC) and the Partnership for Assessment of Readiness for College and Careers (PARCC), have designed CCSS-aligned assessments for students in both math and English language arts at most grade levels. Both groups have second language expert consultants on their development and validation teams. Test designers closely aligned the new standards and the assessments: "This means that the linguistic and academic demands of the new Standards—which in many cases are more rigorous than previous state standards—will also be present in the assessments, which most states require ELLs to take after very limited exemption periods" (Valdés et al., 2014, p. 6). Some states (like Michigan) are developing their own tests that include similar linguistic and academic challenges for multilingual learners.

Federal policy has no set criteria for English language proficiency levels or for redesignation of students as English fluent. These criteria may be established at the state or district level, meaning that students of equivalent proficiency may be placed differently depending on where they attend school (Valdés et al., 2014). One attempt to clarify proficiency expectations has been provided by the World-Class Instructional Design and Assessment consortium (WIDA), which created CCSS-aligned ELD standards for thirty-one states and territories. Other states (like California) have adopted their own ELD standards to align with CCSS expectations. These standards are assessed through tests administered to multilingual students when they first enroll at a school and then annually until their scores indicate they have achieved sufficient English language proficiency to participate fully in grade-level academic work. One challenge for these students is that they must take both content assessments and English language proficiency assessments—twice as many tests as English-fluent students (Valdés et al., 2014).

While is it beyond the scope of this book to challenge national, state, and district testing policies, we argue that individual teachers do have the power to change their classroom assessment practices in order to be accountable to their multilingual students in ways that facilitate students' development of academic language and content learning. Furthermore, while almost all of our multilingual students will still have to take high-stakes tests, what we describe in this book can help them learn the language and literacy they need to perform to the best of their abilities on those tests.

Unpacking the Policy Brief

How do the principles of the ELL Brief connect to these ideas about accountability and assessment? Here we review the relevant sections of the brief and preview how the three teachers at the center of Chapters 3, 4, and 5 incorporated these principles into their day-to-day work of planning, teaching, and assessing multilingual students.

In thinking about equity in terms of helping all students access challenging grade level curricula and demonstrate their learning, it's clear that language is central for multilingual students. Language is how information is communicated, in written and oral forms, so even if students have knowledge of a concept, if they don't have appropriate words in which to express that knowledge, they cannot show what they know. In the section titled "Teaching Language," the ELL Brief stresses, "Second language learners need to develop academic proficiency in English to master content-area subjects" (p. xi). We argue that an equitable approach to helping students develop academic proficiency includes making language explicit through supporting not only students' knowledge *about* grammar and vocabulary but also their ability to *apply* grammar and vocabulary in reading, writing, and speaking.

While we assume that English teachers already have knowledge of the structures of the English language and have experience marking students' writing for errors, we also know that teachers often become frustrated because these practices seem futile—no matter how much grammar you teach and mark, students continue making errors. We hope with this book to introduce an alternative approach to talking about language with *all* students so that multilingual learners especially will develop a contextualized understanding of how words work within sentences and texts. In spite of its esoteric-sounding name, systemic functional linguistics actually provides concrete tools that allow teachers who are not linguists to help students see how grammar functions in the real world, how language is used differently across genres and text types, and how they can use language appropriately in their own writing and communication. Although this book does not provide a complete how-to guide to SFL, we hope that the examples show how its concepts can be integrated into mainstream classrooms without requiring teachers to take on extensive training. We define key concepts in Chapter 2, and then in Chapter 3, we demonstrate how a focus on language allowed Rachel Easton's students to analyze how authors construct arguments by linking ideas within a thesis statement and across a text.

In terms of accessing academic content, reading is an essential but also challenging skill for multilingual students both inside and out of school. Reading in middle and high school is much more than simply decoding letters into words and following stories. As they progress through the grade levels and into college, students need to be able to read increasingly faster and more accurately. They need to be able to understand not only what *is* in the text but also what is *not* included, what the author is suggesting, and what discourses the author draws on. The section of the ELL Brief titled "Teaching Literacy: Reading" recommends including both intensive (close attention to detail) and extensive (focus on reading more) reading in the ELA curriculum. In this book, we describe how the focal teachers use genre-based instruction to provide students with opportunities to read extensively within a given genre and to examine the

Multilingual Student Profile

Junko

Eighth grader Junko moved to Hawai'i with her parents and younger sister when she was ten years old. Her father works for the American branch of his Japanese company, which requires him to stay late at work often. Junko enjoys art and history classes at school but doesn't really like going to her after-school Japanese language classes, where she practices writing essays and reading grade-level books in Japanese in preparation for her family's return to Japan in a few years. Although her father uses English at work, her mother primarily takes care of the children and socializes with other Japanese-speaking mothers whose children are in the after-school language program. As a result, Junko is responsible for interpreting when her mother needs to conduct more complicated transactions at the bank or doctor's office. She frequently reads and translates important mail for her mother as well and sometimes writes responses in English when her mother dictates to her in Japanese.

language features and structures of texts within and across genres through intensive attention to shorter texts. Rather than isolating features in skill exercises and worksheets, the teachers continued to draw on full-length real-world texts as they guided students' understanding of language features within the texts. Concepts from SFL allow teachers and students to discuss these language features in context, build comprehension, and transition from reading to writing. In Chapter 4, we see how Gary Miller's class learned about the concept of voice through analyzing the language of greeting cards and then applied that knowledge to reading literary texts. With such a thorough understanding of how texts are created, multilingual students are better able to understand prompts and tasks on standardized tests and consequently demonstrate their knowledge.

GBI further supports the ELL Brief's assertion that reading and writing are best taught together, through content, with attention to language. The section titled "Teaching Literacy: Writing" provides recommendations for teaching writing that allow ELL students to practice writing in ways that draw on their assets and that give them ways to learn how to write within specific genres. In terms of assessment, collaborative and process writing to widely varied prompts within GBI, accompanied by teacher and peer feedback, gives multilingual students frequent opportunities to see how they are progressing and where they need to practice writing. Just as the ELL Brief recommends that teachers offer explicit and clear feedback on both strengths and areas for improvement, Talia Fenton (in Chapter 6) used formative assessment practices to support her students' collaborative development of a rubric and peer response to written texts.

Revisiting the scenarios at the beginning of the chapter, we see that Vik Singh draws on the principles discussed in the ELL Brief, giving Janice and her classmates multiple opportunities to read real-world texts for a variety of purposes, to collaborate in their writing process, and to share their writing with real audiences beyond the classroom. Vik reads students' writing frequently and offers feedback that helps them know where to make changes as well as where they are succeeding. In her fear of being evaluated based on her students' standardized test scores, Renata McKay, on the other hand, focuses her teaching on preparing students for those same tests. She relies on the textbook for reading assignments and model essays; her writing prompts are based on the year-end timed test, on which students must write individually and without prior preparation. Because the students will not have an opportunity to revise their timed essays, Renata gives them feedback primarily in the form of a score on the district's standardized rubric and a list of the errors they made. It's no wonder that Manuel feels like it isn't worth the effort to try to decode the stories in the textbook or write an essay based on a text he doesn't understand.

Overview of the Book

The purpose of this book is to support mainstream and ESL teachers as well as teachers in other support positions to design language-rich literacy lessons and build formative assessment into daily classroom practices in order to be accountable to their multilingual students. In Chapter 2 we provide a theoretical framework for the teachers' approach to instructional design and assessment: genre-based instruction and systemic functional linguistics. A genre-based instructional focus involves students in thinking critically about texts and their uses for different purposes, audiences, content topics, and contexts. Further, this approach is discovery based, meaning that students are detectives, analysts, and thinkers, as opposed to blank slates receiving teacher-provided information. Used within GBI lessons, SFL gives teachers and students accessible frameworks and terminology for talking about and understanding how language is used in genre-specific ways within the texts they read and write. These interrrelated approaches, while useful for all students, are particularly important for ELLs, who need explicit attention to core language structures in written texts as they develop their receptive and productive English language abilities.

In Chapters 3 through 5, we illustrate how three middle school English teachers designed instructional experiences that included language supports and opportunities for ELL students to think critically and communicate their thinking verbally, in writing, and through other modalities. The teachers we present in these chapters were engaged in ongoing formative assessment to evaluate students' growth and to inform their practices. By documenting growth through portfolios, running records, and regular curriculum-embedded assessments, Rachel, Gary, and Talia collected and shared meaningful evidence that was critical to understanding their students' growth.

In Chapter 6, we return to larger-scale accountability concerns with the performance of ELLs on high-stakes standardized tests. While throughout the book we highlight how teacher practices can support and evaluate multilingual students' learning of the skills and practices emphasized in the new standards, in this chapter we turn specifically to standardized testing and ways that the genre-based instructional focus we discuss can also be employed to prepare students for high-stakes assessments. In wrapping up the book, Chapter 7 takes the classroom principles discussed throughout and shows how teachers can communicate their approach to accountability to stakeholders outside the classroom. We suggest ways that classroom teachers and principals can demonstrate that the ELLs at their school are learning, even if their test scores are not as high as those of other students.

Background on the Scenarios

The three teachers whose classrooms are featured in this book are Rachel Easton, Talia Fenton, and Gary Miller. All three are National Writing Project (NWP) teacher consultants who engaged in a three-year, practice-based professional development opportunity based on the lesson study model for teacher professional development described in Chapter 7. Much of the teaching in the scenarios illustrated in Chapters 3 through 5 was designed and adapted by these teachers (and two others) throughout their involvement with the lesson study. Rachel, Talia, and Gary had each conducted teacher inquiry in an area of writing instruction and were considered by the NWP local affiliate and their school site administrators to be committed to ongoing improvement in writing instruction. The teachers formed a professional learning community to further develop writing pedagogy across their culturally, linguistically, economically, and geographically diverse middle school classrooms. Talia and Rachel both taught eighth grade in urban districts with culturally and linguistically diverse students, most of whom came from low-income communities. Gary taught sixth grade in a small rural school district where most of the English language learners were bilingual L1 Spanish speakers. The diverse classroom settings provided opportunities for the teachers to observe one another teaching in classrooms and communities that varied in community and student demographics. In Chapters 3 through 5, we also reference the invaluable work of the two other teachers in the lesson study, Laura and Elizabeth, whose students were not primarily English language learners and therefore not a focus in this book (see Pella [2011] for more about the teachers and their participation in the lesson study).

As the detailed descriptions of these three teachers' instructional practices show, focusing on language within GBI allows teachers to maintain a level of accountability to their students by explicitly teaching how academic language is used in texts and how texts can be structured for maximum impact on the standardized assessments that are necessary to demonstrate accountability to the school and district. Such an emphasis on language as it is used in real-world texts provides access to content and allows multilingual learners to demonstrate, just as their English-fluent classmates do, what they have learned and what they are able to do through reading, writing, and speaking.

We believe that as teachers view accountability for student learning as a window into their own professional learning, they will understand that practice-based learning models such as lesson study, action research, and collaborative inquiry hold great promise for teachers to develop their knowledge base for teaching English language learners. Providing critical thinking and multimodal learning opportunities for linguistically diverse students was prioritized as teachers planned, taught, and reflected on their language and literacy instruction. The scenarios in Chapters 3, 4, and 5 of this book show the teachers at work, "Giving *all* kids," as Rachel says, "especially ELLs, high-quality learning experiences."

Principles of Accountability for Equity: Talking about Texts and Talking about Language

Teachers who take a genre orientation to writing instruction . . . are concerned with teaching learners how to use language patterns to accomplish coherent, purposeful prose. The central belief here is that we don't just write, we write something to achieve some purpose: it is a way of getting something done.

—Hyland, 2003, p. 18

You're probably reading this book because you wish to bring greater accountability to your work with multilingual students, but you may be unsure where to begin. Equity in education means that multilingual learners in mainstream middle and high school classrooms need access to the same challenging literacy content as their English-fluent peers, but to do so, they also need to learn how the English language is used in specific and varied ways within a wide range of texts. Understanding this diversity of text types for both reading and writing is of even greater importance now, since the Common Core State Standards, as we noted in Chapter 1, shift the focus of teaching away from primarily literary texts toward more diverse informational texts. The CCSS and other new state standards also place greater emphasis on the complex academic language used in texts, pushing students not only to understand the gist of *what* they are reading, but also to analyze *how* authors craft and structure texts and use language to express meaning. These are complicated issues for most teachers and students, but if you have five or six ELLs in a language arts class of thirty students with widely different learning needs, you may be wondering how you can continue to be accountable to all of your students throughout the year.

Being accountable to our multilingual students means ensuring that they have the language and the content knowledge to succeed both in our current classes and beyond. We have found that two interrelated approaches—genre-based instruction and systemic functional linguistics—are particularly successful for differentiating instruction to meet the needs of both multilingual and English-fluent students through providing the explicit focus on language that ELLs need. This chapter introduces key principles and relevant research related to these approaches: GBI focuses on the ways that language varies within and across texts, and SFL helps teachers talk with students specifically about the language used in the texts they are reading and writing.

English language arts teachers are likely to be familiar with GBI as an approach to studying texts or writing for different purposes. In this book, we suggest how it can be amplified with the tools of SFL to make the academic language used to create texts explicit for students who might otherwise not know what to do with these new words and structures. We conclude the chapter with an introduction to the ways our three focal teachers used language-focused GBI to provide ELLs with access to grade-level content and assessments.

Defining *Genre*

As we emphasize throughout this book, being accountable to our multilingual students means helping them access challenging grade-level content and demonstrate their understanding. Learning how texts work, how texts differ, and how authors use language within texts can be difficult for ELLs who have not had as much exposure to written English as their English-fluent peers. Learning to recognize the linguistic and structural differences between and within text types and genres can help students understand authors' decisions and subsequently make their own choices about text structure and the appropriate language to use in their writing. In terms of equity, GBI supports multilingual students in accessing the culturally grounded texts that appear repeatedly in school and beyond.

The term *genre* has many definitions in the world of ELA, potentially leading to confusion in discussions among teachers who may be operating from conflicting interpretations. The CCSS, for example, do not outline writing standards in terms of genres; instead the writing standards are organized into three *text types*:[3] argument, informational/explanatory, and narrative writing. As María Estela Brisk

(2015) points out, each of these labels encompasses multiple, diverse genres, each of which has its own purpose, audience, organization, and language choices. It is more helpful to multilingual students, therefore, to focus less on the genre label and more on what you ask your students to *do* with texts. We therefore draw on the definition of genre developed out of SFL, which categorizes texts as genres by their shared *social and communicative purposes*, *structures*, and *language features*:

> Every genre has a particular number of characteristics that make it different from other genres: a genre has a specific purpose; a particular overall structure; specific linguistic features; and is shared by members of the culture. Most important, members of the culture recognize it as a genre, even though they probably don't use the term. (Gibbons, 2002, p. 53)

A genre . . .

- . . . is recognized by people within a society as serving a particular communicative purpose and

- . . . follows an established structure with specific linguistic features,

BUT ALSO

- . . . varies within itself,

- . . . changes over time and space, and

- . . . contains a variety of rhetorical modes.

The elements of genres, however, are not set in stone:

> Authentic texts tend to be mixed: they often do not follow a rigid format and may contain more than one rhetorical mode. For example, a writer of a memo or legal brief may use definition, narration, and comparison/contrast within the same text product. . . . Genres are related to each other through their purposes, intertextually and contextually. (Johns, 2011, p. 60)

We reconcile these notions with a flexible approach to genre-based instruction.

A Flexible Approach to Genre-Based Instruction

A key factor in GBI is the interactive nature of the process, in which teachers and students analyze existing texts to identify consistent patterns and variable features while creating their own texts in any given text type or genre. GBI promotes the idea that there is no set formula for a genre, but rather that writers choose among various structures and features as they determine the message they want to convey to a particular audience. While this approach helps all students, GBI allows English language learners in particular access to the real world of writing processes while still providing guidelines and support that help them learn how to write in a new language. It also allows teachers to differentiate instruction in ways that support all learners, giving ELLs access to grade-level reading and writing while continuing to challenge fluent English speakers.

We advocate an approach to GBI that encourages young writers to realize the purpose of the texts they read and to produce rather than follow "rule-governed" formats. GBI allows teachers to avoid two unfortunately common and related pitfalls that have been associated with teaching genres:

- Pitfall 1: Instruction and assessment that presuppose that genres have universal (often rigid) structures and a given set of language features that should be imitated. This approach can lead to formulaic teaching of writing and makes text selection from real-world writing contexts and multimodal media nearly impossible.
- Pitfall 2: Following from the first pitfall, the overuse of "prototypical" texts (often written specifically for textbooks) that follow a set organizational structure. Authentic texts in real-world contexts often include a variety of rhetorical moves and have diverse characteristics.

If, for example, we teach how to write statements of purpose for scholarship applications as a series of rule-based structures, students will not realize they have choices about whether to include dialogue in telling their personal stories, or whether to reference their school accomplishments. The texts they create will then sound remarkably similar and often unlike the individual writers' voices. To avoid these pitfalls, we encourage you to think of genre as dynamic and relating more to the social and communicative purpose than to the form of the text. In our view, GBI must be flexible so that we can design opportunities for students to analyze texts for a variety of literary elements, devices, rhetorical moves, language patterns, and structural and other features that bring language into focus. GBI also presents students with a variety of texts that are structured quite differently from one another and include a variety of text features, linguistic features, and styles, but that all serve a similar purpose, such as to argue or to persuade. For example, we see in Chapter 3 how Rachel Easton introduces her students to the genre of arguments through analysis of a speech, song lyrics, a letter, newspaper and magazine articles, a blog post, and excerpts from novels and the school-adopted textbooks. In general, this same process of text analysis can be designed to suit the purposes of any text, be it to present information, reflect on a significant life event, or convince another person to change her or his opinion. This way, we can introduce students to the variety of ways that language is used to achieve different purposes in texts.

You may be familiar with the mentor text approach to genre analysis in which students are guided through the analysis of a text exemplar, prototype, or multiple prototypical exemplars with similar organizational structures and linguistic and other textual features. Students unpack the common features of a mentor text in order to produce their own writing in the same format. Mentor text analysis serves a valuable purpose, especially when examining types of texts that have standard forms, such as haiku, sonnets, some lab reports, or résumés. In the

What genres of literature do you teach in each class? What genres and text types of nonfiction? Which genres are tested on the high-stakes exams your students take?

approach we illustrate in this book, however, you do not need to locate or draft a "prototype" mentor text or exemplar for students to unpack and imitate. Instead, we approach text analysis as a way for students to analyze the various ways that authors can achieve their purposes with language and text structure. In essence, you can use a wide range of texts throughout a genre unit. Therefore, through the rest of this book we refer to our approach to language-focused GBI simply as *text analysis*.

Text Analysis in GBI

Text analysis stems from the idea that in creating a given text, the author had a variety of options. Lessons support students' study of the choices the author made depending on communicative purpose, audience, context, and content; students analyze how authors' choices impact the reader. Rather than working with texts through the lens of a regular and universalized category of structures, we analyze how texts vary according to the decisions made by authors. During a text analysis lesson, students both study individual texts in depth and compare them to other texts in the same genre or text type.

To demonstrate the fundamentals of GBI, let's examine how Shannon led her students through a unit focused on arguing a position and using appropriate relevant evidence to support the argument. To introduce the components of argumentation, Shannon provided her students with various texts about civil rights. Each text argued a position and used relevant evidence, yet each text was also structured quite differently. For example, the students watched a video of a spoken word performance and then read a blog post, a speech, a sermon, and finally a newspaper editorial. Through discussion and close examination of purpose, audience, content, language, and structure of these texts, the students recognized that each text argued a position and supported claims with appropriate and strong use of evidence. However, each text also had a different organizational structure, language features, tone, and register. The class discussed the common components across all of the texts (such as claims, evidence, and reasoning) as well as the differences in language, tone, and structure

Questions to Ask of a Set of Texts

- What is happening in (each part of) these texts?

- How are these texts similar or different? How do you know?

- How are these authors achieving their purposes? How do you know?

- How are the intended audiences, content, and contexts approached in each text? How do you know?

- How would you describe the structure of each text? How are the texts' structures similar and different?

- What language features do you notice? Why do you think the author chose to craft this part of a text in this way?

by drawing on metalanguage (ways of talking about language and texts) they had learned earlier in the term.

A GBI approach to text analysis allows teachers to present texts that look and sound quite different from one another but that include, in this case, the necessary basic structures of an argument (a claim, opinion, or thesis and relevant appropriate and credible evidence). In the preceding example, Shannon selected a variety of texts that featured different modalities, structures, patterns, and language features but that were all arguing a position. Students analyzed each text individually and then made distinctions between and across texts to consider how each author presented an argument and how the particular text was crafted to impact the reader. In this way, students understand that they too have choices to make in structuring their own texts based on their communicative purposes, audiences, and contexts and the arguments they choose to present.

In this approach to text analysis, imitation is allowed but not required, and students gain a sense of texts as containing various rhetorical and structural moves to achieve their communicative purposes. With a shared metalanguage for talking about these moves, multilingual writers gain an explicit understanding of how English grammar and lexicon are used in creating a particular genre or text type. All students, not just those already fluent in English, also have the freedom to innovate and invent new styles of communication as they create texts intended for real audiences. Furthermore, as we illustrate in the classroom-based scenarios in Chapters 3 through 5, students learn how to analyze texts for a wide range of both abstract and concrete features.

Abstract Features of Texts	Concrete Features of Texts
• social process and communicative purpose	• content
• intended audience	• text structure
• context(s)	• text features: headers, sidebars, annotations, graphs, tables, and images
• themes	• language features: word choices, grammar, and mechanics
• tone	• stylistic devices such as figurative language
• mood	
• voice	
• register	

The approach illustrated in this book is based on the notion that there is no set formula for a given text type or genre, but rather that writers make choices as they determine the message they want to convey to a particular audience. The sidebar on page 26 lists some of the abstract and concrete features of texts that can be relevant in GBI analyses of texts. Our approach to text analysis allows English language learners access to the real world of writing processes while still providing them with guidelines that help them learn how to write in a new language.

> Think about ways you already incorporate text analysis into your lessons. How do you scaffold your students' analysis? What features of the text do you focus on?

It's important to remember that multilingual students do have an awareness of genres and text types, particularly if they are literate in their home language. Because they are still developing their understanding of English, however, they may need support in making connections between what they already know about genre and what they need to read or write in English. The ELL Brief recommends, "When possible, include texts in the native languages of the ELLs in the class" (p. xiv). To build on students' existing genre knowledge, teachers can select, or encourage students to bring in, texts in the genre written in their home languages. Through answering the same focal questions (listed on p. 25) about texts in their home languages, multilingual students can develop an understanding of the requirements and variation within the genre as well as how the genre varies across languages and cultures. They can apply this knowledge to English language texts as they work in collaboration with English-fluent peers.

Talking about Language

For multilingual students to delve deeply into the process of genre-based text analysis, they need to both understand and produce the forms of English in which the genres are created. ELLs who have lived in an English-speaking country or studied the language in school may be able to use English for some purposes but may struggle when asked to engage with school-related uses of the language. By definition, most schoolwork—both oral and written—is framed in academic language. Academic language, "the language through which school subjects are taught and assessed" (Schleppegrell & O'Hallaron, 2011, p. 3), is different from how we speak and write in other parts of our lives and includes texts, words, and grammar specific to school tasks. Although the CCSS specifically refer to the "rules of standard English" (Hinkel, 2015, p. 21), we agree with Hinkel that an emphasis on "rules" or a "standard" variety of English is of limited use. More helpful is teaching students how to identify how different varieties of English are used (in and beyond academic settings) and how to deploy language knowledge to understand and create texts that are acceptable in academic contexts. While, as the ELL Brief notes, the specifics of academic language are generally unfamiliar to *all* students, those who enter secondary school classrooms still learning how other types of English work need more explicit attention to how to understand and create texts using the structures and functions of academic language.

To help students learn to use academic language, we need a way to talk *about* language—a set of concepts and tools for showing how language is used in the texts we are reading and discussing in class. Having such a *metalanguage* allows us to draw attention to the ways that academic language differs from and is similar to other forms of English and other languages, as well as how students can use academic language to show their understanding of the content of their subject matter classes. With a shared metalanguage, we can talk with students about how words work in sentences and texts, what patterns we see in the texts, and the ways words and sentences combine to form meaning. Students can also talk about language with one another, supporting and collaborating with their peers in reading and writing projects. Metalanguage allows us to abstract from specific words "to larger categories of meaning that form the grammatical systems of the language" (de Oliveira & Schleppegrell, 2015, p. 97).

One approach comes from systemic functional linguistics, which offers an accessible vocabulary for talking about language with students (Schleppegrell, Greer, & Taylor, 2008) and provides tools to support differentiating and scaffolding literacy instruction for learners of varying language proficiency levels (Gibbons, 2015). These tools allow you and your students to understand how language works in a text and to examine the language used in the texts students are accountable for in school and on standardized tests. While we do not want to make this a book all about SFL (we recommend several resources in the annotated bibliography at the end of this book if you want to learn more), we believe that some understanding of this approach will provide you with a thoughtful alternative to ways of teaching grammar that emphasize rules divorced from meaning—and that will prove more useful to our multilingual students. Here, we provide a brief introduction to concepts of functional language that can be used for talking about and creating texts, as well as explore how SFL breaks language into parts and illustrate some concepts with classroom examples.

One note as you read the following sections: some of the concepts may seem a bit technical at this point. Our advice is to keep reading and thinking about the ideas that underlie the specifics. In the next three chapters, you'll have a chance to see how actual teachers use a focus on language to enhance their approach to genre-based instruction in order to benefit all—but especially their ELL—students.

What Is Language?

SFL emphasizes the functional nature of language—that is, how language is used to perform various functions in society. Moreover, it "emphasizes the interrelatedness between grammar, meaning, and social context. . . . Meaning is not separate from language but is constructed in and through language" (Spycher, 2007, p. 241). Language, according to SFL theorists, is used to create relationships among people and ideas, to represent experience, and to organize texts (Martin & Rose, 2007). SFL furthermore examines the relationships among different levels of language and the linguistic choices that speakers and writers make in order to represent ideas within specific contexts.

How can this approach help in a classroom? Through analysis of the varying ways authors choose to structure texts, students can learn how to make appropriate choices in their own writing: "While specific choices cannot be predicted, patterns of language features can be predicted, and can also be taught" (Hammond, 2006, p. 271). For example, students might read editorial columns from several different newspapers about the same current event. Through an analysis of the texts, they can figure out which elements are traditionally present in editorials (such as a clear statement of the author's opinion and a connection to the current event) and which are optional (such as using quotations from news stories). In this analysis, they also can identify how the authors phrased their opinion statements, whether they used direct or indirect quotations, and what verb tenses they used, among other features. After analyzing the language and rhetorical patterns of texts within a genre, students can then choose from the writing strategies they identified to write their own texts.

Underlying this approach is a big question: what is language? A diagram of nested circles (Figure 2.1) represents the key concepts of how language is used in society. At the core are

Definitions of Functional Language Terminology

- *Discourse:* where grammar intersects with social action (Martin & Rose, 2007); how members of a discipline talk, write, and participate in knowledge construction. This is the level at which language, in the form of text and speech, is used to accomplish communicative or expressive purposes.

- *Register:* levels of formality and choices writers make in creating a text, including topics, relationships between reader and writer, and mode of communication.

- *Lexicon:* the vocabulary of a language, consisting of both content words and functional words. Lexicon includes not only the definitions of words, but also how they are used (collocations) and what they imply (connotations).

- *Grammar:* a system of language forms that offers writers choices in how to convey meaning. Grammar includes clauses, connectors, syntax (word order), parts of speech (how words function in sentences), and verb tenses and aspects, among other things.

- *Metalanguage:* terminology for and ways of talking about how language is used for specific purposes (de Oliveira & Schleppegrell, 2015; Moore & Schleppegrell, 2014).

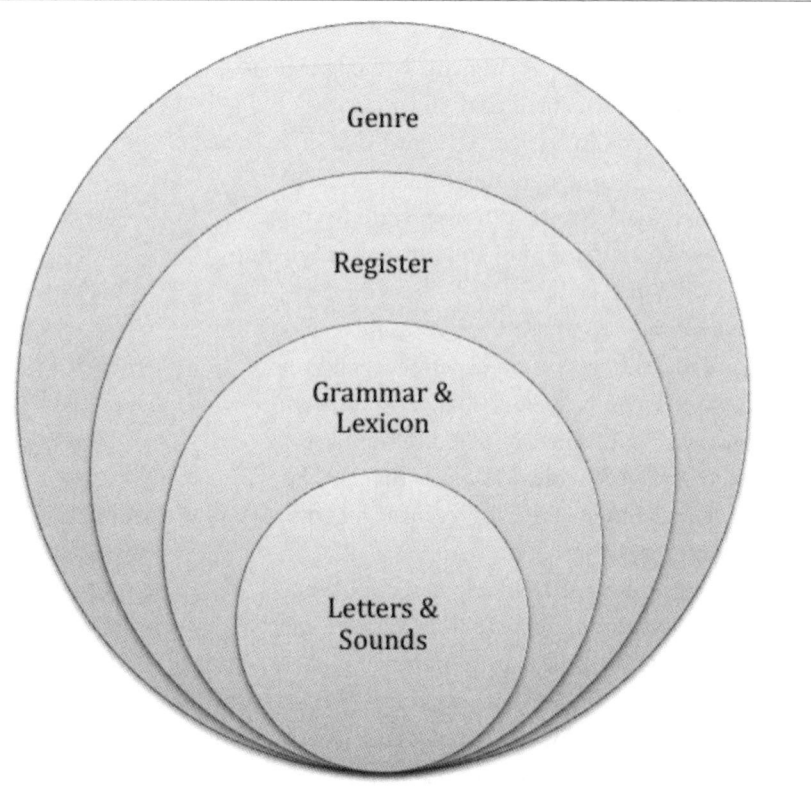

Figure 2.1. Key concepts in language use (after Martin, 1997).

the small pieces that make up every utterance or sentence: *letters and sounds* that can be combined to make up words, phrases, and clauses. At the next level—*lexicon* and *grammar*, also called *lexicogrammar*—the focus is on words and meaning. *Lexicon*, or word knowledge, includes knowing the definitions of words, but also the connotations and collocations—what words mean within different contexts and how they are used in combination with other words. These are not just content words (what we often think of as vocabulary), but also the functional words (such as articles, conjunctions, or pronouns) that connect content words to make meaning. Individual words alone cannot represent meaning; they can only do so when embedded in grammatical sentences (Brisk, 2015). As *grammar*, words are combined to make phrases (strings of words) and clauses (complete thoughts, with subject and verb). Clauses present *processes* (verb groups), *participants* (noun groups), and *circumstances* (adverbials), which together convey meaning (Brisk, 2015).

Many approaches to teaching language stop at this point, focusing on the rules of combining words into "correct" sentences. An SFL approach, however, promotes emphasis on the bigger picture aspects of language: how grammatical resources are used to convey messages within society. These higher levels begin with *register*, which represents the intersection between language and context and may be familiar as a term for explaining levels of formality in texts. Register is also how authors indicate their stance on their topic, their level of confidence in what they are writing, and their relationship with readers (Gibbons, 2015). Focusing on register allows for talk about how authors choose to use lexical and grammatical resources to shape their texts for particular purposes. In other words, the way we speak or write depends on why we are speaking or writing and to whom. An emailed note inviting your friend to coffee, for example, will use different grammar, word choices, and structure than an official report written for your principal.

The outermost circle of the diagram in Figure 2.1, encompassing all the other levels of language and register, is *genre*. From an SFL perspective, genre "is a staged, goal-oriented social process. Social because we participate in genres with other people; goal-oriented because we use genres to get things done; staged because it usually takes us a few steps to reach our goal" (Martin & Rose, 2007, p. 8). Language appears in patterns that are repeated within social contexts; those repeated patterns of language are what constitute a genre of text. As we noted earlier, genres represent generally accepted properties of texts, but these properties vary and evolve over time (Schleppegrell, 2004). For example, the register and structure of a procedural text are different when comparing a science report with a recipe, and a recipe written in 1800 uses different grammatical structures and lexical choices than a modern recipe. Register and genre are determined by the discourses in which a person is writing or speaking. Discipline-specific discourses have distinctive features or ways of structuring oral or written language (text structures) that provide useful ways for the content to be communicated.

We focus on genre-based instruction as a means to both guide and assess multilingual learners' development of academic language and literacy. By maintaining an awareness of and emphasis on all the levels of language, we can help our multilingual students learn to make connections between the words an author uses and the author's purpose in writing. Within any real-world genre, authors make a wide range of lexical and grammatical choices. Through talking explicitly about the language choices authors (including themselves and their peers) make, multilingual students can develop an understanding of not only what a text means, but also how to create texts on their own.

How Can Teachers Use SFL Tools with ELLs?

One challenge for teachers in making academic language explicit for ELLs is knowing how to talk about words and clauses. SFL supports the development of a shared metalanguage between teachers and students. Having a set of words and phrases that label text types and language functions allows students to understand the purpose and content of written genres (Schleppegrell, 2010). With this meta-language, teachers and students can make explicit the ways that texts are similar or different, why writers selected certain words over other words, and what linguistic resources connect ideas across texts. Research has shown that, contrary to a popular belief that it would confuse them, even young English language learners can understand and make use of grammatical metalanguage (Dare, 2010). You don't need to know all the technical terminology used in linguistics in order to develop a shared metalanguage with your students; what is important is being consistent and understanding the concepts behind the labels you use.

Let's look at how a teacher might use SFL tools in a classroom, in this case in a seventh-grade unit on folktales. In preparation for writing their own stories, the class could examine the language of a story from Brazil, "Why the Bananas Belong to the Monkey."[4] The text uses some complex sentences and archaic phrases that could prove challenging to English language learners. This particular story also includes many sentences with pronouns, including the "dummy subjects" *there* and *it* in existential clauses. After reviewing three metalanguage terms—*participants* (which the teacher explains are the people and things doing and receiving the main actions), *processes* (the actions of the story), and *circumstances* (phrases that tell more about the processes and describe participants)—the teacher and students could begin dividing sentences using the graphic organizer in Figure 2.2 (modeled after de Oliveira & Schleppegrell [2015] and Spycher [2007]) to identify how language is used in the first paragraph of the story.

By filling in this graphic organizer together (on the board or using a projector), the teacher and the students can begin to analyze how texts are created through the use of participants, processes, and circumstances; how connectors are used to link ideas; and how ideas build on one another through the use of pronouns that refer back to nouns. Using just the metalanguage terms *processes*, *participants*, and *circumstances*, the students learn to talk about core grammatical concepts and recognize variations in sentence structure. In the text in Figure 2.2, for example, students can trace the character of the old woman from her first introduction ("a little old woman") to continued reference to her ("the old woman") to the pronoun ("she"). Students can also see how the processes in the story begin with descriptions, repeatedly using "there was," but then changes to actions ("she made" and "the monkey gathered"). The information in the first column further allows for an analysis of the ways that clauses are linked. You may have noticed that the process

Figure 2.2. Clause analysis graphic organizer.

	Connector	Participant	Process	Participant	Circumstances
1	Once upon a time when	the world	had (just) been made		
2	and	there	was	only one kind of banana, but very many kinds of monkeys,	
3		there	was	a little old woman	
4		who	had	a big garden	full of banana trees.
5		It	was		very difficult
6	for	the old woman	to gather	the bananas	herself,
7	so	she	made	a bargain	with the largest monkey.
8		She	told	him	
9	that if	he	would gather	the bunches of bananas	for her
10		she	would give	him half	of them.
11		The monkey	gathered	the bananas.	

(verb) in line 6 is in the infinitive (the *to* form); helping students learn which connectors hold clauses (complete sentences) together and which introduce phrases (such as the *for* in line 6) can further support students' development of control over the complex sentences valued in academic language. Focusing on a grammar point of relevance to English language learners whose home language does not require a word in the subject column (such as Spanish), this organizer can help illustrate the need for *there* and *it* dummy subjects when the meaning of the sentence is carried in the information after the verb. Laying out sentences in a table like this can help them notice that English requires a word in the subject column, even if it doesn't mean anything.

After working through the first paragraph as a group, the teacher could then assign pairs of students to analyze sections of the rest of the story, making sure that each ELL has an opportunity to work with fluent English speakers who can explain or model their understanding of participants and processes. The students could work collaboratively and then share their completed graphic organizers with the class.

The teacher might then direct the students to focus on the process column for the next activity, analyzing the verbs for their functions in the story. The class can discuss how some verbs describe a physical action, while others report on what people think or say, and still others connect the subject to a description. The metalanguage they choose as a class comes out of their discussion, not a grammar book, and uses high-frequency words that all the students know well.

Figure 2.3. Process (verb) analysis.

Action	Thinking/Feeling	Saying	Being/Having
To tell about events	*To report on the "inner world" of the writer*	*To construct dialogue or report on the words of others*	*To construct relationships, definitions, and descriptions*
Had been made Would gather/ gathered Would give Passed Saw	Thought	Told Called Said Answered Shouted	Was Had

This second graphic organizer, Figure 2.3 (adapted from Spycher, 2007), adds more metalanguage to the class's discussion of grammar as students learn to classify the processes they found from the first organizer. By thinking about the different types of processes, they analyze not just the surface meaning of individual words, but also how those words work within the context of the story. In this example, with words drawn from the same story, students can see that the author mainly used *action* and *saying* verbs, indicating that the focus was on surface processes rather than characters' feelings or relationships. After the class collaboratively analyzes the verbs in the folktale, the teacher could create a word wall in the classroom where the students add the processes they have found into the appropriate columns. Comparing this text with another text written for different purposes (perhaps a science or social studies text about bananas) can give students an understanding of how different genres and registers are constructed.

While such a close analysis of a text may initially seem time consuming and impossible to fit into an already hectic course plan, it has considerable benefit for both ELLs and fluent English speakers alike, all of whom are still learning academic uses of language, particularly for reading and writing. Rather than starting with a lecture on a grammar point or using a worksheet with isolated sentences, discussions about language are grounded in specific texts. Students can provide examples from the text to support claims about voice (choices of vocabulary, for example) or other aspects of language; this then allows them to learn abstract literary concepts from experience rather than as memorized definitions (Hammond, 2006). Multilingual students have reported that learning these processes helped them approach reading complex texts confidently and independently (Spycher, 2007). In terms of time management, once you have taught the initial text analysis process, for example, you can assign small groups of students to analyze different portions of the text and report back to the class. They could compile a master list of processes that could be shared on a poster for the whole class to use in their own writing (Schleppegrell, 2010).

With this ability to analyze the words and grammar of texts, students can identify, understand, and create texts within myriad genres and text types. They can use the metalanguage they develop through text analysis to assess one another's texts as well through peer response based on a grounded understanding of the purpose of the text (Schleppegrell, 2010). Expanding their consideration of language beyond the classroom, students can study language variation within their own communities or within multiple texts on the same topic but written for different audiences (Derewianka & Jones, 2010). The teachers whose classrooms we examine in detail in Chapters 3 through 5 demonstrate other ways to support students' access to and learning of many language features as part of their study of genre. If you are interested in learning more, we recommend that you check out some of the useful resources we discuss in Chapter 7 and the annotated bibliography at the end of this book.

The processes of language and text analysis we explore allow students to figure out what each section of a text is doing and how each rhetorical move made by the author contributes to the overall impact of the piece. We contend that when students have engaged in text analysis using language-focused GBI all year, by test-taking season they will be better prepared to unpack assessment prompts for their purpose and expectations, figure out what the task is asking them to do, and respond with appropriate organizational structures and language. Writing prompts and performance tasks themselves might be considered a genre because they share basic procedural features and expectations and serve a communicative purpose (to demonstrate understanding of content). We delve much more deeply into this important concept in Chapter 6.

Language Objectives, Language Demands, and Language Supports

Knowing about GBI and language analysis is an essential first step to using these tools in your teaching. To make them work in the classroom, however, you need to integrate them into your daily planning by writing language objectives for both unit and lesson plans to maintain accountability for the learning of the multilingual students in your classroom.

As we have noted previously, a key factor in equitable instruction for English language learners is making language explicit and contextualized in real-world texts. To bring the language of the curriculum into focus, you can begin by identifying the *language demands* for the tasks and texts in a lesson or unit of study, particularly the academic language, because it is the means by which students develop and express content understanding. Academic language represents both the general and the specialized disciplinary language that students need to understand in order to participate and engage meaningfully in the content area. Students learn that academic language involves registers of English used for specific purposes in both writing and speaking, and that it is different from social conversation. Teaching academic language is far more than just instructing students in "correct" usage or vocabulary.

Language demands can be broken down by thinking about the same nested levels of language discussed earlier in this chapter: discourse (genre and register), lexicon and grammar, and letters and sounds. To identify language demands for a given lesson or unit, focus on specific ways that students use academic language (including vocabulary, function words, levels of formality, and word order or syntax) to participate in the learning task through reading, writing, listening, and/or speaking to access content and demonstrate their understanding. Figure 2.4 lists some of the language features that may be relevant to lessons you currently teach. Which language features you select as the focus of a lesson will depend on individual students' levels of English proficiency and on the relevance or necessity of those features to students' participation in the lesson's content objectives. Additional suggestions can be found in the resources provided in Himmel (2012), Lindahl and Watkins (2014), and the Stanford Center for Assessment, Learning, and Equity (2016).

Letters and Sounds
- Spelling rules and exceptions
- Shapes of letters (print, italics, and script/cursive)
- Pronunciation of individual letters and dipthongs (combinations of letters)

Grammar
- Sentence structure: clause components (processes, participants, and circumstances) and complexity
- Types of sentences: statements, questions, commands, exclamations, etc.
- Language functions: articles, verb tense, prepositional phrases, etc.
- Syntax: word order, including transitional words and connectives that perform specific functions

Lexicon
- General academic vocabulary used across disciplines (e.g., *compare, analyze, evaluate*)
- Discipline-specific words (e.g., *constitutional, nucleus, polynomial*)
- Words and phrases with discipline-specific meanings that differ from meanings used in everyday life (e.g., *table, cell*)
- Abstract high-frequency words
- Word study: how words are structured, including word families and prefixes, suffixes, and roots, and how to figure out meanings of unknown words

Discourse
- Register: how grammar and lexicon are combined (and not combined) for a particular usage in a particular discipline and context
- Modality: how writers express their stance and degree of certainty through choice of words
- Genre: how texts are structured (using register, grammar, and lexicon resources) to enact a specific communicative and social purpose
- Writing: context awareness (cultural, social, geographic), paragraphing, design
- Reading comprehension: prior knowledge about topic and genre, questioning strategies, anticipation

Figure 2.4. Identifying language features for writing language objectives.

How does this approach of connecting language to texts work in the classroom? Here's how our three focal teachers proceeded. During their lesson study professional development planning process, Rachel Easton, Gary Miller, and Talia Fenton discussed ways that GBI as an approach to text analysis might support students in investigating texts for more than content. They developed lessons and units in which students analyzed texts for purpose, audience, content, and context within and across genres. Using metalanguage derived from SFL, this genre-based approach provided a uniquely language-focused opportunity for literacy learning in all disciplinary content areas.

In writing language objectives to accompany their content objectives, the teachers acknowledged that their ELL students needed to learn how to access new concepts and how to relay their understanding of those new concepts orally and in writing. The teachers engaged in a collaborative process called "backwards planning." They began by articulating the student learning goals and desired outcomes and then carefully selected relevant, rigorous, high-interest texts for adolescent readers. Next, they identified the language demands of the texts and accompanying reading, writing, listening, and speaking tasks. They considered the metalanguage they needed to teach the lessons, keeping in mind the complexity of both texts and tasks in relation to the specific students present in their classrooms. To identify the language demands, the teachers asked themselves the following questions about what students needed to *do* to access reading, writing, listening, and speaking in the unit:

1. Which words might cause students difficulty (reading silently or aloud) due to their spelling? Which words contain less common combinations of letters? Which words are homophones (words with the same sound that are spelled in different ways depending on their meanings) or homographs (words with the same spelling that are pronounced differently depending on meaning)? These language demands are the *letter and sound* issues.

2. What content-specific terms might need attention? Which familiar words are used in a different way than students are used to? Which idiomatic phrases are important to the meaning of the text or the discipline? Which verbs signal writers to particular ways of thinking about the task?[5] These are the *lexicon* concerns.

3. What types of structures will students encounter at the word, sentence, paragraph, and whole-text levels? For example, does the text contain connectives and transitional language? Long, complex sentences? Passive or active voice? Is there nominalization (verbs and adjectives turned into more abstract noun forms, as is common in history and science) in the text? These are the *grammar* considerations.

4. How is the message of the text communicated? What is the register of the text? Is it in multimedia, print, or oral mode? What are some organizing

features of the text? What is happening in each part of the text and how does each part of the text relate to the whole? How does the author convey his or her stance on the topic of the text? These language demands are the *discourse* foci.

After identifying all the possible language demands, the teachers then took an inventory of what they knew about their multilingual learners, considering what they had already learned and what they most urgently needed to know to access the content of the lesson. They selected a manageable number of points from this list to create language objectives for their instructional units. With those objectives in mind, the teachers determined which instructional strategies could be used to draw explicit attention to the language features students needed to learn.

As you can imagine, there will be overlap in the four areas, but it is important to tease them apart first in order to anticipate what areas may need close attention. This process helps you bring the language into focus and design ways to support students in seeing the language and developing metalinguistic awareness. The key consideration is to target the specific language supports to match the language objectives.

In Chapters 3, 4, and 5, overview tables break down the teachers' planning processes, and the classroom illustrations take you through some of the ways they used a genre-based approach and SFL tools to bring the language into focus for the English language learners in their classrooms. Each chapter begins with a unit overview that is followed by a closer look at how each teacher identified the language demands and designed language supports to meet the language objectives of their lessons. In Chapter 3, in preparation for a unit on analyzing arguments, Rachel's class, instead of analyzing one specific text structure, discovers discourse-level variations in a wide variety of texts (song lyrics, blog posts, speeches, editorials, poetry, and visual images) for a focus on the many ways an argument can be presented. In Chapter 4, Gary's students are analyzing various visual and print texts, including greeting cards, to uncover how the author used language, images, and text structure to express a particular voice. In Chapter 5, Talia engages students in the analysis of ways to integrate evidence into written texts, as well as the analysis of their own and one another's texts in a peer feedback revision activity. While all three teachers used GBI in similar ways, we have chosen a different lens for each chapter to emphasize particular aspects of their accountability to their multilingual students.

Teaching for Accountability and Equity

Classroom Illustration: Text Analysis and Argument Writing

Chapter Three

I want them to be engaged in figuring it out. I don't want to just tell them the answers. I want to adapt for my ELL kids, what I know other kids—those who [will] get into the best colleges and have the best jobs—are learning.

—Rachel

Meet Rachel Easton, a seventh- and eighth-grade teacher in a high-poverty urban school whose students are all English language learners from diverse linguistic backgrounds. In this chapter, we observe how she engaged her students in the analysis of texts to support their language and literacy development. While all of the students in Rachel's English language arts classes are classified as English language learners, much of what she does as a teacher would transfer to a mainstream class with fewer ELLs. Rachel, as you will see, draws on the concepts we introduced in the last chapter (genre-based instruction and systemic functional linguistics) to help her students learn to analyze texts in support of their own literacy development. We examine Rachel's teaching through a focus on the discourse level of language, looking in particular at how she guided her students to analyze how texts work for different purposes, audiences, contexts, and content.

The classroom-based snapshots of the lessons illustrated in this chapter come from a larger unit of study, spanning approximately six weeks, that focused on analyzing argument texts. The class examined the texts for the author's purpose, intended audience, contexts, content, text structure, language features, and linguistic complexity. During the unit, students engaged in text analysis to build their knowledge of some of the academic language (and metalanguage) needed to structure, discuss, and write an argument on a topic of their own choosing. In this chapter, you will read excerpts from a series of lessons in which students analyzed a wide variety of texts (speeches, video, visual images, song lyrics, newspaper and magazine articles, blog posts, and excerpts from novels and the school-adopted textbooks). Throughout the text analysis processes, they wrote short responses (chart notes, anecdotes, reflections, brief narratives, summaries, and other short informational writing). Along the way, as a key aspect of their analysis of texts, Rachel included targeted opportunities for students to unpack the language and structures of texts, to draft multiple responses to texts, and to share their ideas and opinions about the subjects and content of the texts they encountered.

In these chapter illustrations, you'll see how Rachel carefully planned the learning experiences and language supports for her students by focusing on the forms of language students would need in order to access the content—an important component of teaching ELLs. Throughout the unit, she included frequent opportunities to observe and assess her students' understanding of the content and their ability to use academic language appropriately. Table 3.1 provides an overview of the larger unit of study from which the snapshots are drawn. The format is adapted from the book *Understanding by Design* (Wiggins & McTighe, 2011) and illustrates Rachel's backwards-planning process, from desired student learning outcomes to her day-to-day lesson planning. Table 3.2 is a magnified look at the language objectives listed in the first part of Table 3.1 in Rachel's genre-based unit of study.

In this unit, Rachel was looking for every opportunity to explicitly teach language so students could access challenging grade-level and age-appropriate content. She was dedicated to equity teaching and provided access to content through a variety of language-focused, collaborative, and explicit teaching approaches. Table 3.2 shows how Rachel identified and unpacked some of the essential language demands of the unit in order to articulate language objectives and build in language supports throughout the unit. Consider Table 3.2 as a magnified view of the unit-level Language Objectives in Table 3.1. In her planning process, Rachel articulated at least one language objective per lesson along the lines of the examples in Table 3.2.

Table 3.1. Unit Overview: Text Analysis and Argument Writing

What are the desired outcomes for my students?

Students' analyses of arguments in different modalities and forms support their oral and written communication of an argument on a topic and in a format of their own choosing. Students explain how their text analyses impact their writing choices and process.

Common Core State Standard(s): Reading 1–10, Writing 1, 4–10

California ELD Standards—Interacting in Meaningful Ways, Learning about How English Works, Using Foundational Literacy Skills

Language Objectives—students learn and operationalize the academic language demands of reading, writing, listening, and speaking about arguments. (See Table 3.2 for a magnified view of language demands, sample language objectives, and language supports.)
- Lexicon: metalanguage for talking about arguments and text structure
- Grammar: complex sentences using connectors and verbs to indicate causality
- Discourse: varied text structures of argument genres and text types

Students will know that:	Students will (do):
Authors make stylistic, structural/organizational, language, and content choices based on purpose, audience, and contexts.	Read and interpret texts from different authors written for a variety of audiences, contexts, and purposes
The analysis of various texts can support writing decisions.	Locate and explain how a given text is crafted to express an author's intended goals
Writing opinion/persuasive pieces and arguments differ, yet all require varying degrees of reasoned judgment, logical reasoning, and relevant evidence.	Use information from the analysis of texts to plan, draft, revise, and communicate their written and spoken arguments
Authors use some aspect of ethos, pathos, and/or logos to reason through their arguments. Various types of data (anecdotes, statistical evidence, examples, etc.) can support a position.	Unpack the language of texts to learn how texts work and how English works
	Use the language of the discipline to communicate thinking effectively

How will I assess students along the way?	
Formative Assessments	**Summative Performance Tasks:**
Short written responses and discussions	Draft and revise a written argument
Notes handouts	Reflection on experiences
Investigation station handouts	Verbal explanations of thinking
Annotation of texts	
Group posters	**Other:**
Short responses to text analysis questions	Running records
Daily reflections	Observation tools
Text-to-text analysis—graphic organizers	Interview notes
Draft of argument	Audio recordings
Peer conferencing sheets	Portfolios
Reflections on incorporating feedback	

Table 3.2. Meeting Language Objectives: Identifying and Supporting Language Demands

Language Demands: Lexicon	Language Supports: Lexicon
Metalanguage for talking about arguments: • Position • Thesis • Refute • Counterargument • Evidence, data • Claim, Counterclaim • Audience • Purpose • Context • Message • Intention • Persuade • Support • Cite • Inform *Sample language objective: locate and highlight components of an argument (in a given text set) using metalanguage: e.g., author's position, claim, evidence, support, and call to action.*	Word wall with icons and visuals Word lists: new vocabulary students write in a "tool kit" section of their "writer's notebooks" Visuals for each word in the tool kit Choral practice: group repetition of complex words, terms, and phrases to practice pronunciation Digital photography: photos of students as they engaged in each lesson and used the pictures to lead warm-ups, discussions, and reflective conversations each day Teacher modeling: using each term and supporting student participation in a "try it" for each term Think-aloud process: reviewing the text under a document camera to unpack complex language in context by breaking down words, sentences, and punctuation and using context and other clues to determine word meanings
Language Demands: Grammar	**Language Supports: Grammar**
Syntax: longer and more complex sentences structured to make and support an argument; connectives used to extend sentences Nominalizations: noun forms of actions that are expressed as verbs in less academic contexts Pronouns: noting how texts shift from using proper nouns to pronouns *Sample language objective: notice and explain instances of nominalization across the text sets.*	Modeling complex sentence unpacking: document camera and teacher-created videos used for think-aloud and class discussion about sentence structure and word choices "Try it" activity: students arrange and rearrange mixed-up sentences (individual words and phrases printed on strips of paper) and explain the differences when shifting words and punctuation around in a complex sentence. Collaborative text examination: use document camera and class discussion of ways that authors use nominalization of verbs to condense ideas and for how pronouns are used to refer back to previously mentioned ideas.

Table 3.2. Continued

Language Demands: Discourse	Language Supports: Discourse
Selection of a variety of texts within argument/persuasive genres that include different registers and structures: • Compare/contrast • Problem/solution • Sequential order • Cause/effect Additional texts, including the following structures: • Beginning with a lead (hook, attention grabber) • Stating the author's position, provide background on the topic • Using evidence and analysis • Concluding with a call to action Other texts containing all of the features listed above but in a different order: • Delayed thesis and beginning with facts, evidence, and built toward the position in the conclusion • Variety of types of evidence used to support the positions: facts and statistics; anecdotal and testimonial reasoning *Sample language objective: identify the text structure across a text set using metalanguage: cause/effect, problem/solution, topic/evidence/analysis, or other.*	Model text annotation: use document camera to model the process for highlighting sections of text, annotating each section, and making notes identifying the rhetorical moves and purpose of each section. Q&A: targeted questions to unpack each section of the text and optional sentence frames for each answer. Visuals and graphic organizers that define text structures common to informational texts: • Compare/contrast • Problem/solution • Sequential order • Cause/effect • Other

General Language Supports

Academic discussion cards and templates with sentence frames for engaging in an academic conversation[6]

Posters with discussion terms (agree, disagree, clarify, support, extend) and student-generated sentence frames for each discussion term

Practice and scaffolding through use of the cards, sentence frames, templates, and genre-specific metalanguage such as *argument, critique, book review, short story, play, poem,* etc.

Charts and posters for students to practice informal writing during the investigation stations

Handouts for the investigation stations with each question clearly written and room for responses. Each handout has sentence frames on the back as an option but not a requirement.

Checklists and running records for formative assessment of students as they engage in tasks and language development

Daily warm-ups, reviews, and reflections

Digital photography of students as they engage in the work to prompt discussion and reflection

Exit tickets focused on a word or language function used each day

As you'll see in the pages that follow, Rachel's lessons ranged from building background and language knowledge to analyzing and writing argument texts. In keeping with a GBI-focus, Rachel's lessons engaged students in reading real-world texts and analyzing how the authors used language to structure convincing arguments. Through hands-on experiences with the concepts, her students developed a shared understanding of metalanguage for talking about arguments, which they then applied to reading and writing academic texts. Rachel identified texts far in advance of these lessons and spent time with her colleagues in the lesson study to analyze each text for topic, purpose, audience, context, and content as well as text structures, language features, and forms of linguistic complexity. For example, she carefully selected texts and noted where they contained nominalization, modals, complex sentences with shifting pronouns, connectives, and a variety of types of text organization and structure.[7] Also important to these lessons is the emphasis she placed from the beginning of the year on writing groups, peer response, and a variety of multimodal activities centered on writing for at least two hours a week. The lessons illustrated in this chapter include:

- Archaeology Activity: Building the Field for Academic Language
- Investigating Arguments: Author's Position
- Connecting Back to Language Experiences: Using Metalanguage
- Investigating Arguments: Evidence, Support, Reasoning
- Investigating Arguments: Organizational Structure
- Investigating Arguments: Language Use

Classroom Snapshot 1

Archaeology Activity: Building the Field for Academic Language

To build some background knowledge around several essential language functions and academic vocabulary, Rachel planned an experiential learning activity that she called the "archaeology activity," in which students played the role of archaeologists from the future charged with analyzing artifacts in order to make claims about Americans in 2015. Rachel designed this series of lessons to provide language experiences around several language functions: analyzing, describing, generalizing, and arguing. Students were provided an opportunity to collect and analyze data and operationalize some of the metalanguage needed to analyze written arguments.

Rachel's archaeology activity proceeded in the following steps:

> 1. Image analysis: Rachel projected images, visual texts that depicted archaeologists working in the field and interacting with multiple artifacts. Students analyzed the images and discussed what archaeologists do and how they draw conclusions about society and culture from physi-

cal objects. Rachel noted action verbs such as *analyze, describe, hypothesize,* and *generalize* on wall charts for later reference.

2. Trash artifact "data" analysis: In groups of four, students played the role of archaeologists from the future, investigating the lives of people in twenty-first-century America. As archaeologists, they began by "unearthing" and analyzing trash artifacts, which came from teacher-prepared "trash artifact" bags that included the following items: an empty water bottle, clean fast food containers,[8] a cleaning product, an empty aspirin or other medicine container, something with a recycling logo on it, an empty diet soda can, and something with a bar code.

3. Drawing conclusions: Students described and analyzed each artifact and wrote notes on their graphic organizers (see Figure 3.1) in response to three questions that guided them from simple description to inductive analysis. (Note that this is the same process students used when analyzing the images of archeologists, with increasingly higher-order thinking questions.)

4. Comparing ideas: After making notes on their handouts in small groups, students shared their ideas with one another and then with the whole class, one artifact at a time. Rachel charted all responses on posters and saved them for future reference.

Figure 3.1. Handout for recording data: archaeology activity.

Artifact	Analyze one artifact at a time. Describe what it looks like; what the label says; and the size, color, or other physical attributes.	What do you think the people who used this artifact did with it? What makes you think this?	What do you think this artifact says about the general population? Make a generalization about this society. Why do you think this?
Tylenol container			
Fast food bag (Happy Meal)			
Water bottle			
Aluminum diet soda can			
Shampoo bottle			

Figure 3.2. Sentence frames for discussion.

The artifacts show that in 2015 America was _____ because _____.
     The evidence suggests _____ because _____.
     The data shows _____ because _____.
I agree that _____ because _____.
While I agree that _____, I also think _____.
I disagree that _____ because _____.
     Can you please clarify what you mean by _____?
     Can you give me some evidence to support your claim about _____?

5. Making claims about twenty-first-century America: Students referred back to the charts that Rachel had created during the class discussion about each artifact and brainstormed some general claims about twenty-first-century American culture based on their artifact analysis. Rachel modeled how to state a claim with a fill-in-the-blank sentence frame: "I think the culture was <u>environmentally conscious</u> because they had <u>recyclable materials</u>." As a resource, she provided additional sentence frames for discussion (see Figure 3.2).

6. Each group of students suggested a claim. Rachel encouraged some debate so that all students had a chance to negotiate how to make generalizations based either on the totality of the artifacts or on a select few. Each student provided a written claim statement using a sentence frame as an exit ticket (which also served as a formative assessment).

The archaeology activity accomplished a variety of things: students developed schema, or background knowledge, about how to use information from data to form an idea or make a claim. They were exposed to and began to use some of the metalanguage necessary for investigating texts: *analyzing, describing, generalizing, evaluating,* and *arguing.* Students additionally got experience stating an original claim based on evidence from the trash artifact analysis. The archaeology activity scaffold provided some language resources for discussing how to use language to accomplish intended purposes: in this case, stating a position and supporting the position with evidence.

This activity was adapted from an approach described in George Hillocks's book *Teaching Argument Writing, Grades 6–12* (2011), in which secondary English students encounter a fictitious "lunchroom murder," examine evidence, and formulate a position about the incident. According to Hillocks, when introducing students to the complexities involved in analyzing and crafting arguments, it's a good idea, before moving into researching complex texts, for students to negotiate the components and language of arguments with high-interest, accessible content. To do this, you can introduce some form of problem, case, scenario, conflict, inquiry, or controversy and position students as problem solvers, consultants, scientists, mathematicians, historians, detectives, or, as described here, archaeologists. These problem-centered experiences frontload metalanguage and key academic vocabulary in accessible contexts. Students are challenged to engage in disciplinary thinking and build background knowledge. They also learn that people in every discipline and walk of life (including, and especially, students like them) are critical thinkers with a unique contribution to make.

Classroom Snapshot 2

Investigating Arguments: Author's Position

After having the concrete experience of drawing on archaeological evidence to make claims, Rachel's students were ready to take on the more abstract work of analyzing claims in a variety of texts in order to see how texts work to accomplish an author's intended purpose. They moved through several phases of text analysis in an activity that Rachel called "investigation stations." In the investigation stations, the students analyzed a variety of written and visual arguments so they could develop the language and schema necessary to read and comprehend written arguments as well as to craft and produce their own arguments.

By first participating in the archaeology activity, students had an opportunity to use concrete data to draw their own conclusions. Rachel told her class, "I want you to believe in your own knowledge. I want you to see yourselves and your own thoughts as valid." She explained, "In our next few lessons, you will discover some of the traditional features of arguments and discuss why certain features of arguments are more effective than others in certain social contexts."

On a daily basis, Rachel unpacked academic language with her students in order to give them a metalanguage for discussing and analyzing texts. For example, in this lesson, Rachel unpacked the terms *social context* and *traditional* with her students. The following discussion is from Rachel's introduction of the term *traditional*.

Rachel asked, "So what does the word *traditional* mean?"

One student responded, "Like a religion or a holiday or a family tradition?"

Rachel confirmed the student's contribution. "Yes, the root word is *tradition*. A tradition is a noun that means continuing beliefs or practices across generations." She then asked, "How many of you have a family tradition?"

Most students raised their hands.

Rachel then asked, "What kinds of family traditions do you have?"

The students responded with stories of reunions, celebrations, holidays, and religious ceremonies, among others.

Rachel probed, "Why are these events called 'traditional'?"

Several students suggested, "Because they are things we do as a family over and over again from generation to generation."

Rachel confirmed their contributions. "Yes, because these traditions are continuing patterns, they are consistent from generation to generation." She wrote *tradition* and *traditional* on the board. "What is the difference between these two words?"

The class called out, "The ending *-al*."

Rachel pulled the students toward her language goal. "When the noun *tradition* is changed to an adjective describing an event, what happened to the word?"

Many students called out, "The ending *-al* is added."

Rachel finished the discussion with some additional grammar commentary. "Right. When some nouns are changed to adjectives, the ending *-al* is added. So, just like the traditional holidays and events that you have in your family, there are traditions in writing too. Some kinds of writing are traditional because there are common practices that are continued across types of writing, just like a tradition is followed in your family—there are traditions in writing too. We're going to look at some writing and try to figure out what they have in common—in other words, what are the *traditional features* of this type of writing?"

Although Rachel didn't do so at this point, this discussion could also be an opportunity to build students' lexical and grammatical knowledge by creating a reference chart with other words that end in *-al* and other endings when changed from nouns to adjectives, such as *natural* or *factual*.

In the investigation station lesson, Rachel posted the argument texts that she and her colleagues had carefully selected. Some of the texts were enlarged and taped to the wall, and visual images and videos were presented in media stations on laptops. The argument texts in the investigation stations included a speech, song lyrics, a letter, newspaper and magazine articles, a blog post, and excerpts from novels and the school-adopted textbooks. All texts presented and supported a position and expressed an argument.

As the investigation station lesson began, Rachel explained to her students, "Today we're going to do an investigation station. When you look around the room, you'll see exhibits, just like in an art gallery. In our room today, each exhibit is a text. Some texts are printed and taped to the walls, and some are multimedia, so you'll have to use the laptops to view those." Rachel reminded students that they were detectives and enlisted their help to investigate the arguments for both similar and different features.

Throughout each of the investigation stations, Rachel used the theme song from *Mission Impossible* to signal when to move from exhibit to exhibit. As befitted the occasion, she wore a lab coat and carried a large magnifying glass to encourage her students to act as detectives. In this way, her lesson was designed to scaffold critical thinking for and about reading and writing, not simply to scaffold reading and writing tasks. Rachel supported her students' higher-order thinking processes by creating collaborative activities like these that provided opportunities for language development and use.

Students moved through the classroom gallery in their ongoing writing groups. Together, the groups analyzed each text, presented across various genres and modalities, as an argument. At each station, a group read, listened to, or viewed a text and analyzed it based on a series of questions that Rachel and the teachers in the lesson study group had designed. Handouts for each argument text posed the following questions:

1. What is the topic of this text?
2. What is the purpose of the piece?
3. Who is the intended audience?
4. How is the text structured?
5. Describe the author's position: what is the author arguing in the piece?
6. How do you know?

After the students had examined the texts[9] and returned to their seats, Rachel engaged the class in small-group discussions to determine what was similar and different across texts. She asked groups to volunteer a response to each question orally and wrote their responses on chart paper, creating one chart for each text. She began, "Let's go through each text, one at a time, and answer all of the questions together as a class. But first, what did you notice was similar for all of the texts that you investigated? What was different?"

The students responded that the differences included the types of text. They also noted similarities across the texts, namely that they all expressed an opinion or viewpoint of some kind—an argument. However, in response to the questions about topic and author's positions, purposes, and audiences, students' answers were vague and without much elaboration. Rachel could see that her students understood the main purpose of this first exercise: to note that even though each text was in a different mode, they each expressed an argument. The texts had something important in common. Rachel determined, however, that her students needed to practice deeper analysis of the same texts.

She designed the next lesson as a continuation of the first investigation station lesson. Each writing group was assigned one text that had been exhibited in the investigation stations. Students negotiated with the members of their group to describe the central argument of their assigned text. Each group was given the piece of chart paper created during the teacher-led debrief and was invited to expand on what was currently on the chart by responding to the following prompt: *How does the author get his or her message across?*

Each group added to the chart paper for their text. For example, one group wrote, "The author's argument sounds casual in the blog post because they are trying to express themselves to their peers about things that matter to their lives—not write in a formal way." Another group noted, "The message in the picture is more about the way they are trying to say something through colors or what they put in their art. Their message is their position." A third group suggested, "A formal argument is made in the article because the author is writing in a professional way to an audience that knows a lot about the topic."

Rachel debriefed this part of the lesson by explaining, "I see that each group explained a different way that the author got his or her message across. Some of you said things like 'the message was casual, or formal, professional sounding,' while others wrote that the message was conveyed through colors, as in the visual art, or with sound and pictures in the animated video. These are the differences, yes, so now I'd like to focus on the similar features of each text."

Rachel hung the chart paper back up on the walls, and students walked around the room in a second investigation looking for features that showed up in every text. Throughout this process, Rachel floated around the room taking notes, documenting students' discussions and participation in running records, while supporting and prompting students. One form of support she provided was a set of sentence frames students could use if they wanted to. For example, the discussion frames in Figure 3.2 were used to support students in agreeing, disagreeing, asking clarifying questions, and stating their opinion. In this way, students who felt confident in their language ability could experiment with new sentences, while those who were just starting out could still frame their discussions in an academic way.

The discovery-based nature of the investigation stations supported students in analyzing the similarities, or *traditions*, of argument texts as well as the differences among arguments in a variety of forms. The main goal was for students to understand that even though the modes were different, the traditional features of an argument include a claim or position about a topic, evidence to support the position, and a call to action of some kind. By the end of this investigation lesson, students were able to see some of these traditional features across each of the texts. According to Rachel, "I wanted to see what kids came up with themselves before I taught them anything. I wanted to experiment with ways to analyze arguments so I could see where to go next. I wanted to see where they would go with it first instead of trying to clearly define it for them."

In debriefing the second investigation station activity, Rachel explained to her students, "When you're exploring or investigating something, you're not always coming up with answers that are correct. That's okay. It's the journey in doing that yourselves that's going to help you learn how texts work and how language works in texts." Rachel had deliberately designed the text analysis lessons as openended investigations of arguments that she had carefully selected; she reminded her students throughout the lesson that "there is no *one* right answer when you investigate; you analyze, and when you analyze, you should be focused on trying to figure things out."

After her lessons that day, Rachel reviewed her notes and realized, "They still need more support, so next I'll debrief this activity with the whole class by brainstorming with them and creating a list of what they believe a position is, as opposed to the topic of the argument. . . . I'll do a mini-lesson where we analyze a model, and I'll do a think-aloud where I distinguish between the *topic* of the text and the *position* of the author to remind them what they are looking for and how to do it." As a result of her analysis of student learning from that lesson, Rachel designed the subsequent lessons for further investigation of similarities and differences across texts. She recognized her accountability to her students' learning and her awareness that some had not yet mastered the central objective of her text structure lesson. As opposed to watering down the process or overly scaffolding her students' learning, Rachel wanted to maintain the rigorous nature of text analysis in a way that both supported and challenged her students.

Classroom Snapshot 3

Connecting Back to Language Experiences: Using Metalanguage

Informed by her observations and notes from the previous lessons, Rachel made some adjustments to her lesson plans. She began the next text analysis lesson by reflecting back to the archaeology activity, reminding her students of the ways they had functioned in that lesson as archeologists by *analyzing, evaluating, describing, generalizing*, and *discussing* ideas about the trash artifacts. She wanted her students to make connections between acting as detectives to investigate arguments in the investigation stations and their archaeology role-play experiences. Projecting pictures she had taken of them working during the archaeology activity, Rachel asked, "What were you doing in these pictures?" The students discussed what they were doing with a partner while Rachel encouraged them to use the process metalanguage *analyze, describe, discuss, evaluate*, and *generalize*, which she had posted clearly on the wall with visuals for each word as a reference. Then she projected pictures of them in the investigation stations and in their writing groups working at their desks to chart notes. Rachel continued, "What were you doing in these pictures?

What is similar? What is different?" She encouraged students to use the words *argument, text, investigate, collaborate, think, write, read, describe, discuss,* and *analyze* (among other terms posted on a chart labeled Academic Language Processes) as they responded to her discussion prompts.

After the whole-class discussion of the connection between the archaeology role-play and the investigation stations, Rachel placed a short editorial about bike helmet laws on the document camera. She modeled a think-aloud process by talking about the distinction between the topic of the text (bike safety) and the author's position on the issue (that bike helmet laws should be instituted and actively enforced). Some of that think-aloud is captured in the following vignette.

Rachel introduced her process to the class: "First, I'll read through the text out loud, and then I'll stop and tell you what I'm thinking as I'm reading. This is called a *think-aloud,* and I am doing this to show you what I do when I read a text and try to figure things out about it. Hmmm." Rachel read and highlighted a line from the text. "I think this line is telling me what this text is *about*. The *topic* of the text is what the text is *about*. Let me read this line again: 'Bike safety is critical to the health and well-being of a bike-loving community.' I think this text is going to be about *bike safety*. Let me continue reading. Oh, here is another important line. 'Many communities seek to improve the environment, and as a result, have a lot of bike lanes, and in those lanes, bike riders. Communities need to make sure that they have bike safety measures in place.' Class, do these sentences seem like they're starting to tell us what this text is going to be about?"

The students agreed. One explained, "Yes, because the text is talking about being a safe place to ride bikes."

Rachel continued to read. "Okay, let's assume for now that the *topic* of the text is *bike safety*. This may change, but for now let's go with that. Hmmm. . . . What is the *position* that the author is taking on bike safety? How many of you, thumbs up or down, think the author is *for* bike safety?"

All the students put their thumbs up.

Rachel accepted their responses. "Yes, I agree. Most people are not really against being safe. Let's see if the author's *position* gets more specific than the topic that bike safety is important." She read aloud again and stopped to highlight a line, *Wearing a bike helmet is the first and most important thing a bicyclist can do to promote bike safety.* Rachel exclaimed, "Aha! I think this is the author's position. Thumbs up if you think this is the same as the topic. Or is it different?"

Several students responded, "Different because the topic is bike safety, but the position is that in order to be safe, bike riders should wear their helmets. The position is about wearing a helmet. The topic is about bike safety." Rachel continued highlighting more lines to help students see the differences between a topic and an author's position on that topic.

Next, Rachel demonstrated how to transfer this kind of thinking onto a graphic organizer, which she had previously created as a document on her laptop and projected onto the screen. The chart was a simple table with four columns labeled Topic, Author's Position, Evidence, and Call to Action. In this modeling process, Rachel was able to unpack the text, copying and pasting from the editorial sentence by sentence, and place sections on the chart. She began this visual text analysis process by copying and pasting the sentences from the text that provided background on the topic under the section of the chart labeled Topic. She copied and pasted the sentences that offered the author's position on the section of the chart labeled Author's Position, and continued until the text was transferred to all four columns. As she unpacked each new sentence, Rachel enlisted the students' help to decide where each section of text belonged in the chart. For example, for the sentence *Helmet use has been estimated to reduce head injury risk by 85 percent*, Rachel asked a series of questions, pausing after each one so the students could respond: "What column does this sentence belong under? Why? What type of evidence is this? How does this support the author's position?" The students suggested that the sentence was a form of evidence, since it gave a statistic about how bike helmets reduced injuries and therefore showed the value of helmets. If a sentence could go in more than one section, that too was discussed and negotiated. This process was an interactive and visual way to show her students how to analyze texts in order to understand how they work to express an argument. Rachel planned this lesson to preview some of the traditional ways that authors craft arguments, such as by providing background on the topic, making position statements, using evidence, and ending with a call to action.

After deconstructing the editorial on bike safety with her students, Rachel planned the next day's lesson. She wanted to provide opportunities for her students to return to the argument texts from the investigation stations and apply some of the metalanguage used in the deconstruction of the editorial: *topic, position, claim, evidence, audience, purpose, context, data, reasons, conclusion*, etc. To this end, the next lesson included a closer read of the texts from the investigation stations. Rachel divided the class into two groups; half of the writing groups stood by their text and the chart they had created earlier in response to the questions on their graphic organizer handouts. The other half of the class participated as audience members. Each group presented its chart and engaged in discussion with their audience. When all the presenting groups had spoken, the groups switched, allowing the audience to become presenters. The poster session–style presentation was an opportunity for Rachel to hear students using the unit's metalanguage so she could further assess their progress in talking about arguments. For example, as the students explained the topic of their text, the author's position, and the evidence the author presented, many changed their minds and revised their charts as a result of some of the interactions they had with classmates. By listening and prompting students with questions, Rachel was able to determine that they were ready for the next text analysis lesson: analyzing the examples, reasons, or evidence the author used to support a position.

Classroom Snapshot 4

Investigating Arguments: Evidence, Support, and Reasoning

In preparation for the next step of the text analysis activity, Rachel taped new chart paper around the room. On each empty piece of chart paper, she wrote the title of a text and the position of the author (as previously determined by the students). She posted the chart paper on the wall next to the associated text. In their writing groups, students again went around the classroom and investigated the same texts they had previously analyzed in the investigation stations. However, this lesson introduced a new lens: Rachel wanted students to analyze texts for increasingly complex features, a central aspect of close reading. It was important to keep the same texts as the vehicles for analysis but change the investigative lens so that each time students returned to the text, they could focus on what they were looking for, instead of trying to understand new content. Therefore, in this lesson, Rachel directed students to investigate the types of evidence, reasoning, or data the authors used to support their positions. In each investigation station, students worked with a handout listing the following questions for the station's text:

1. What types of evidence does the author present to support his or her position?
2. How well do you think the evidence supports the position?
3. How does the author craft the structure of the text?
4. How do you know?

Rachel began by leading the students in brainstorming a list of ways that authors might support an argument. She transcribed the students' suggestions on a piece of chart paper, prompting, explaining, and providing examples for each. Students used this chart as a resource during the investigation station:

Some Ways to Support an Argument
- Facts: scientific facts, historical events
- Numerical data: statistics, calculations
- Quotes from experts, reasoned judgment
- Examples
- Anecdotes and testimonials (personal experiences)

After discussing the various ways authors might support an argument, the students engaged in the investigation stations to discover the types of evidence used in each text. Having responded to the questions for each text, the students returned to their desks in their writing groups with the chart from their group's previously assigned text. As experts on their assigned text, the groups were tasked to negotiate how the rest of the class had interpreted the way the author supported his or her position. Each group discussed the contents of the chart, added their own thoughts, and decided how they would present their assigned text to the class. A short share-out from each group opened up room for whole-class discussion, culminating in a teacher-led debrief.

This series of lessons was powerful for Rachel's students. She told the class at the beginning of her debrief process, "We are asking you—junior high students— to do something really hard: respect one another. You are learning that when you have differences, you learn how to work through them, and to compromise. That's a huge skill in itself that could last you a whole lifetime." Beyond these interpersonal skills, however, the students were also learning foundational academic literacy practices they will need as they move through high school and college and into the adult world. By teaching them how to apply metalanguage for talking about texts such as *purpose, audience, topic, evidence, position*, and *organizational structure*, Rachel was fulfilling her accountability to her ELL students who otherwise might not have the linguistic tools to access these complex real-world texts.

Classroom Snapshot 5

Investigating Arguments: Organizational Structure

In the next lesson, Rachel invited her students to focus on the craft and structure of each of the texts they had been reading in the earlier investigation stations. Because Rachel valued preparing her students for real-world writing, she had selected arguments that were communicated differently across modalities and text types. Her deliberate choice of dissimilar argumentative texts is part of the flexible nature of genre-based instruction. In other words, she was interested in continuing to develop her ELL students' understandings of some traditional features within *arguing* as a social communicative process (an opinion, position, or claim supported by credible, relevant evidence), even as the argument texts took different forms. Having focused thus far on two of the traditional features of argumentation—stating a position and supporting that position—Rachel believed her students would be better prepared to develop their own arguments with a deeper look at craft and structure.

Rachel began this lesson by telling her students, "I'm going to just push you into the water today instead of letting you stick in your toes and get used to the temperature." This introduction got their attention, and she continued, "I want to go deeper into our study of arguments by investigating text structure. We're going to stay in our role as detectives today, just like we did when we explored some of the traditional features of arguments in our other investigation stations. Today, though, we're going to investigate each of the arguments for something called *text structure*." To help students understand the meaning behind the metalanguage, Rachel projected a picture of a play structure that could be part of any playground. She asked the students, "Before we begin today, let's get together and define our terms. What is this called in your community?"

The students responded with *climber, slides, playground,* and *park,* among other terms.

Rachel asked, "Does anyone call this a *play structure*?"

The students replied, "Yes!"

Rachel queried, "Why do you think this is called a play structure? Let's look at the two words separately. *Play. Structure.* Why *play*?"

Some students suggested, "Because you *play* on it."

"Okay. Why *structure*?"

The students variously offered, "So it won't fall down. It is strong. It's made, so it's a structure."

Rachel confirmed their suggestions, "Exactly! A structure holds everything together and keeps it from falling apart. Where else do you see structures?"

The students noted houses, buildings, roof, plumbing, and other locations.

"What do you think it means to have structure in a text?" Rachel asked.

Some students replied, "To keep it together so it doesn't fall apart."

"Yes—just like the play structure or the structure of a building, texts have structures too. These structures organize the text and keep it together. Are all play structures the same?"

"No," the class called out in unison.

Rachel probed, "What are some differences?"

The students noted some differences: some are big, some are small, and some have slides, ropes, bridges, swings, or tire swings.

Rachel explained, "Just like play structures, texts also have different structures. Why would the structures be different in a play structure?"

The students suggested that some are for little kids, while others are more challenging for older kids.

"Now you're talking!" Rachel exclaimed. "It's the same for text structures. An author decides how to structure a text by thinking about who will read the text, just like a play structure designer thinks about who will play on the structure before designing the play structure. Writers also structure texts based on their purposes—what they want the texts to do. Is this also the same for a play structure?"

"Yes, because you can do all different kinds of things on play structures if they're designed that way."

"Excellent. So now that we understand text structure as the way a text is organized around its purposes and audience, we're going back to your same texts and we're going to analyze them for their structure. We're going to look at the structure and think about how the authors made these choices based on their purposes and who they expected their audience to be."

Rachel reminded the students that it was important to read each of the texts again before addressing the questions she had given them. Under the document camera, she previewed images of four possible text structures: problem/solution, cause/effect, compare/contrast, and order/sequence. Rachel also asked two questions to guide her students back to the texts:

1. What is the overall structure of the text?

2. How do you know?

As they returned to the texts in the investigation stations, students could enlist one of their group members to read the text aloud while the others looked at the possible text structures listed on a handout for clues. Later, explaining her thinking while planning this aspect of the lesson, Rachel said that she wanted to "clearly define terms with kids and tap into their prior knowledge to do that. Every time we encounter a new academic term, I try to find something familiar to them so they can relate to the term. So far that has worked quite well for my students' understanding of *traditional* and *structure* as these terms relate to academic writing. I also try to frontload not only the process for the lesson and the logistics, but also the purpose." Rachel felt strongly that her students should understand the purpose for their lessons before, during, and after their learning. She explained, "They need to buy in. I don't like to keep these things a mystery, because that's not fair. The thing that I worry about is that I am asking them to read and comprehend what they read and look at a question and understand the question, and that is a lot when you are learning a language."

Much like the previous text analysis lessons, in this investigation station, students worked with their writing groups to analyze the structure of the same text they had previously been assigned. (Rachel now considered the groups to be the "experts" on their texts.) In their writing groups, the students first determined the structure of their text and then proceeded through the classroom stations to investigate the other texts for structure. This way, they had some practice first with a very familiar text, as experts, before encountering the other texts. In the investigation stations, students investigated the structure for each text with their text structure handouts and the two questions to guide their analysis.

As we noted earlier, the structure for each text was different. Each text also presented an argument around a different topic, in a different context, with a different purpose and intended audience. Each of the arguments that Rachel had selected was accessible to middle school readers, and Rachel thought her students would be interested in the topics. Knowing her students' language proficiency and interests was part of the success of the lessons. According to literacy scholar Heather Lattimer, "Using well-selected texts in a genre study is essential. Nothing can cripple a lesson faster than a text that is not age appropriate, reading-level appropriate, or above all, engaging to the students" (2003, p. 16). Rachel's chosen texts displayed varying organizational structures, but all were arguments and as such included a position and support for the position.

After students had analyzed each text for its structure in the investigation stations, Rachel led a whole-group debrief. During the debrief, she noticed that her students were accessing some but not all of the features of each text's structure. As a result, she planned a teacher-led lesson for the next day, unpacking several of the texts from the investigation stations via the document camera. Rachel placed each text under the camera and went through it section by section, asking students:

What is this section of the text *saying*?

What is this section of the text *doing*?

How does each section of the text contribute to the overall structure of the text?

Why do you think the author chose this structure?

As the class debriefed each question, Rachel posted charts on the wall with lists of reasons for structuring texts in different ways. This lesson provided visual access to text structure and reinforced students' use of metalanguage such as *organization, paragraph, problem/solution, cause and effect, sequential order, compare/contrast, claim, support,* and *evidence*.

In this scenario, Rachel wanted to see what her students could do first (around identifying text structure) before she directly taught new concepts. There are both benefits and potential drawbacks to this approach. One positive result is that Rachel was able to see how her students engaged in the tasks, allowing her to determine where to support and challenge them. A potential drawback is that the direct instruction came after their attempts to undertake a complicated task. This could mean that students have to un-learn something in order to re-learn it. Both approaches have value. Think about this: How do you see Rachel assessing her students' knowledge and readjusting her teaching? How might you do this in your own classroom?

Classroom Snapshot 6

Investigating Arguments: Language Use

The next set of lessons in the unit focused on investigating how language can be used to present an argument. Rachel's students engaged in another investigation station with their writing groups. We have seen how Rachel's students closely read and analyzed eight texts through the following lenses: purpose, audience, topic, authors' position, evidence, and text structure. In other lessons (not described in this book), they had also investigated the texts for the following: introducing and refuting counterarguments; figurative language; ethos, logos, and pathos; and some recurrent text features such as tables and graphs, image captions, subtitles, headers, and sidebars. The students had further investigated the authors' use of transitions, time order and signal words, and voice.

In this final investigation station lesson, students explored the texts for targeted language features. Rachel created handouts for students with questions about language:

1. What types of connectives are used in this argument?
2. What is each of the connectives doing?
3. How do you know?
4. Are there any complex sentences that need unpacking? Highlight puzzling sentences for whole-class discussion.
5. Is there nominalization present? Highlight puzzling words for whole-class discussion.

In preparation for this investigation station, Rachel previewed the metalanguage terms *connectives*, *complex sentences*, and *nominalization* by selecting sentences from the investigation station texts. On her document camera, she deconstructed the selected sentences with her students. For example, she noted these two sentences that the students had identified as puzzling:

1. *No country in the world relies as heavily on democratic elections to promote justice as the United States of America.*
2. *The destruction of the earth in terms of pollution, unsustainability, and waste is unconscionable.*

"Let's start with the first sentence," Rachel began. "Notice how the phrase 'democratic elections' is used here as a noun. When you go to vote in a democratic election—let's say to vote for president—the election is an event, place, or thing, so it is what?"

The class called out, "A noun."

Rachel agreed. "Yes, an election is a noun." She wrote *election* on the board

and underlined the *-tion*. "However, when you go into the booth and do the action—the verb—what are you doing in that booth?"

"Voting. Electing the president."

Rachel confirmed, "That's right." She wrote *electing* on the board and underlined *-ing*. "So you see here how the author of this sentence changed a verb, *to elect*
or *electing* a president, into a noun by adding the *-tion* to make the noun *election*.
This is called *nominalization*. Notice how *election* and *electing* have the same root,
elect. Let's pay attention to the ends of words, or the suffixes, and see if we can see a
pattern. Let's look at the next sentence that you said was puzzling."

Rachel pointed out the second sentence: *The destruction of the earth in terms
of pollution, unsustainability, and waste is unconscionable.* "What do you notice about
some of the word endings in this sentence? Do you see any suffixes that might be a
clue?"

The students called out several words: *pollu*tion, *unsustainab*ility, and *destruc*-
tion.

Rachel accepted their suggestions. "Yes, let's go through these words one at a
time. *Pollution*." She wrote the word on the board. "Is this a noun or a verb?"

The students all recognized it as a noun.

"How do you know?" Rachel asked.

Some students noted, "Because it is a *thing* that has happened to the earth."

"Okay, is there a verb associated with the noun *pollution*?"

"Yes, *pollutes* or *polluting*."

Rachel agreed and wrote *polluting* on the board. "Right—so here again we see
the suffix *-tion* changing a verb that ends in *-ing* into a noun. Do you see a pattern?"

The students noted that it was the same as changing *electing* to *election*.

Rachel went through the same process with *destruction*, *destroy*, and *destroying*
and then moved on to *unsustainability* and unpacked it in the same way, pointing
out both the prefix *un-* and the suffix *-ability* and working with her students to understand the verb *sustain*. Note that in this lesson, Rachel is using traditional grammar terminology (*noun* and *verb*) rather than SFL's broader labels *participant* and
process. When textbooks or standardized tests use these labels, remaining consistent
can help students, as long as the teaching that introduces the terms makes clear
connections to the *functions* of the concepts and how they are used in real texts,
rather than just to abstract definitions and examples divorced from their communicative purposes.

Finally, Rachel wanted to point out another way to look for a clue about
nominalization. "Now that we've looked closely at how words change by adding
prefixes and suffixes, there's something else that is happening in this sentence." She
underlined the word *of*. "Let's look at this very small word *of* living in this sentence

with so many long complicated words. This little word *of* does something very important that gives us a clue to nominalization. What is the word *of* doing here?"

The students noted that it tells us what was destroyed.

Rachel agreed, "Yes, when *of* is present between nouns or noun phrases, like in this sentence, *of* is between <u>destruction</u> *of* <u>the earth."</u> She underlined the nouns in the sentence. "This gives us a clue that one or more of the nouns here came from a verb. How do we know this?"

The students explained, "Because the *of* shows that the destruction was *of* the earth because it happened to the earth, because one did something to the other."

The next investigation station focused on looking closely at each of the texts for connectives, complex sentences, and nominalization. Students highlighted puzzling sentences and words from each text, and Rachel led the class in deconstructing some of the sentences the students had identified as difficult.

The next day, Rachel reviewed the previous day's lessons with several genre-themed questions that further drew on the metalanguage students had encountered throughout the unit. For example, reviewing the lesson from the day before, Rachel asked, "Which texts have nominalization and which don't? Why do you think these more academic texts have more complex language? Who is the audience? What are the purposes? Why do you think the blog posts were written in first person, but the published article in *Science* magazine was in third person? Why do you think the letter is in first person but the editorial is in third person?" Leading students through this discussion helped them see that an author's language choices, including the degree of linguistic complexity, reflect the goals, audience, purpose, context, and content of the author's arguments.

Reflection: Accountability through Built-In Formative Assessment

Rachel used formative assessments throughout her teaching and documented a variety of ways students engaged in participation and learning. Throughout the investigation station lessons, she floated around the room with a clipboard to record notes and make running records of student participation and academic language use. She stopped often to check for students' understandings and to prompt them to think further about and discuss aspects of the texts. For example, during one of the investigation stations, Rachel engaged in a conversation with her student Seng, a Hmong speaker who had lived in the United States for only a couple of years. She noticed that he had been silent in his group, so she prompted the group to ask him for his ideas and opinions. She later explained her reasoning: "Not just Seng, but all of my kids need to talk about what they read. I think they would be more confident about their writing if they could spend more time talking about it first."

She learned from her discussion with Seng that one of the texts contained content that was unfamiliar to him. The text was a petition to the principal created by a student who argued against teacher interference in the way kids dance at school dances. Seng explained to Rachel that he had never been to a school dance and that after school he went straight home to help his family. This was critical information for Rachel and informed her text selection approach because she recognized that many of her students' lives outside of school were different from that of her own teenage daughter. Cultural unfamiliarity can interfere with multilingual students' comprehension of texts that are otherwise linguistically appropriate.

The investigation station activity also engaged students in collaborative learning, which may not be the first choice for every student. Seng was also an example of a quiet student for whom this sort of social learning activity might be outside of his comfort zone. Nevertheless, Rachel was able to access valuable information by talking with Seng and observing him as he participated in the interactive activities. This information fostered her understanding of Seng and her other students. By engaging students in activities that encourage them to think about and discuss texts with one another, Rachel was able to gather data to inform her next instructional steps. Such information gathering about student learning is a key part of professional accountability. Rachel described how she used reflection and formative assessment from interacting with her students and from observing them in action:

> It was good to try to get them to separate out their opinion from the opinions of others and even from the opinion of the author. I was really psyched when Kevin said, "Well, I just want to say I agree with this one [the position in a given text] but the second one's argument [in another text] is stronger." I love that I heard him say this because we were evaluating the strength of the evidence to support the position in this exercise, not whether or not we agree with the argument. This was essential because I knew that the kids in that group had some experience in that activity separating their own opinion from those of the author.

When asked specifically which forms of formative assessment were most useful to her, Rachel replied, "Seeing them in action was the most important." In the snapshots described in this chapter, Rachel held herself accountable for assessing not only her students' academic language development, but also their feelings of inclusion and empowerment. For example, at the end of the first investigation station illustrated in this chapter, Rachel explained what she had observed:

> I noticed that one group in particular were all saying to each other things like, "OK, so what do you think? OK, so what do you think? Why do you think that?" That was really off on another level. They aren't all fluent in English, and yet they are high achieving because they interact. They seem to feel really comfortable with each other.

When we have done this before, they were always asking for me to check their work. They always ask, "Check this is . . . is this right? Am I doing this right?" The good news is . . . they weren't saying that to *me* this time. Even as I was walking around, none of them said, "Check this . . . is this right?" That was really good. I do think they are [still] concerned with the right answer, but this is a closer step to validating their own ideas. I want them to feel comfortable and free and open and I want them to really feel like it is all focused on them—their ideas—like when they are exploring and investigating. Tomorrow I am going to turn it into a debate because one group can say, "This [argument] was strong," and the other group can say, "This [argument] was weak," and then we can start to look at the "Why?" and then I can ask, "How well did you explain it?" and then later in the unit I am going to tie it all back to their own writing.

From Reading to Writing: Drafting Arguments

The archaeology activity described in the beginning of this chapter positioned students in the role of archaeologists from the future. In this role, they uncovered and analyzed trash artifacts from twenty-first-century America and brainstormed claims about the culture based on what they found. Some of the claims included the following:

- American culture in 2015 was technologically savvy.
- Americans in 2015 were environmentally conscious.
- People in America in 2015 must have been lazy.
- In 2015 Americans did not care about the environment.

One goal for this first part of Rachel's unit on arguments was to support students in operationalizing some academic metalanguage for discussing text analysis processes, including *analyze, describe, evaluate,* and *generalize.* Another goal was to practice interpreting data in order to make a claim.

In closing the unit of study on arguments, Rachel returned to the archaeology activity. She reviewed what they had investigated as archaeologists, linked that investigation to some of the work they had done in the investigation stations, and used data collected during the archaeology activity to co-construct with students an original written argument in order to scaffold and prepare students for writing arguments on topics of their own choosing. The unit gave students the opportunity to use their written argument as a springboard to express and support their position in a medium of their choosing such as video, poetry, speech, visual images, or cartoons.

We realize there are many ways to approach lesson sequencing. Rachel decided to bookend her text analysis lessons with the archaeology activity. However, she could have co-written an argument with her students immediately after engaging in the analysis of artifacts. Another option would have been to build in short spurts of writing after each text analysis lesson. This way, students could build an argument based on the archaeology artifacts as they engaged in each part of the investigation station. For example, after the first investigation station where students analyzed the authors' positions, they could have returned to their notes from the archaeology activity to draft their own positions. Then, after examining various ways authors used evidence to support their positions in the second investigation station, students could have selected the evidence from their notes that most accurately supported their own positions. After looking at a variety of text structures, students could have determined a structure that made sense to their overall purposes. Finally, after analyzing the language of the texts, students could have added, revised, and strengthened the language of their arguments. Any approach is effective as long as it reinforces the idea that writing is an iterative process of thinking, writing, reading, writing, discussing, writing, revising, writing, etc.

How do you sequence your writing lessons? How do you integrate reading, writing, speaking, and listening? How do you introduce drafting into your writing process? Do your students read about topics first, use mentor texts, and then begin to draft? Or do they draft in smaller increments throughout your reading and text analysis processes? *How might these approaches benefit your English learners?*

In this chapter, we see Rachel introduce some academic metalanguage and analytical processes during the archaeology activity. She ended that initial piece after students had brainstormed some possible claims they could make about America in 2015. After the archaeology activity, we followed Rachel through the close reading of eight argument texts in the text analysis investigation station lessons. She then used the archaeology activity to co-construct an argument with the whole class to scaffold the next step, which involved students in producing a written argument around a self-selected and researched topic.

No matter how you decide to lead students through the process of crafting an argument, text analysis is most beneficial when the compelling foci are revisited throughout the reading and writing process. In other words, regularly referencing the text analysis charts, handouts, rubrics, sentence frames, language ideas, lists of terms, and discussions from the investigation stations supports students as they bridge from the text analysis activities to their own writing. These practices reflect teachers' accountability to the students in their classes because they are ways to help students experience firsthand the processes of identifying what is important in a written text and choosing the appropriate language to create their own texts in response. While some fluent English speakers may be able to notice unique features and replicate them in their own writing, ELLs and other struggling writers are often overwhelmed by the sheer quantity of new features in a text and do not have the prior experience with English language texts, or the foundational lexical and grammatical knowledge, to pull out the features that make a particular genre different from other genres. The many varied activities that develop students' awareness of text features at all the levels of language we discussed in Chapter 2, therefore, provide ELLs equitable access to the grade-level material being used in mainstream classrooms.

While the overall unit of study described in this chapter was based on the analysis of arguments, it could just as easily have been adapted to focus on the analysis of a different genre or text type, such as reflective recount, critique, book review, or feature article. As an alternative to organizing units of study around genres, they could be planned around themes, such as the American dream, coming of age, or immigration.. Furthermore, conceptual units of study can focus on concepts such as sustainability, conflict, or oppression. In this chapter, we present a unit of study focused on *arguing* as a social communicative process or genre. But whatever the focus, language-focused GBI can be infused into any unit of study with an emphasis on text analysis, which calls for a wide range of reading, writing, listening, speaking, language use, and language development across a variety of text types, modalities, and genres (for further reading, see Brisk, 2015, and Smagorinsky, 2008). The appendix starting on page 149 provides guidelines for your own planning, teaching, and assessment processes.

In Chapter 4, we see how Gary leads his English language learners through a variety of text analysis activities around *voice*. Although many of the text analysis activities Gary does are similar to those Rachel used, in our discussion of Gary's teaching, we shift our focus from the big picture (discourse level) ideas about how texts work to focus in on writers' specific language choices (the lexicon and grammar level). Then in Chapter 5, we foreground Talia's formative assessment work as she engages her English learners in language-rich literacy tasks such as reading and responding to literature. In each of these scenarios, teachers are focused on equity teaching by providing rich language and literacy experiences to their English language learners. The teachers' flexible approach to genre-based instruction promotes language-focused lessons, which provide access to challenging learning experiences for ELLs. They pay particular attention to language development and use throughout their lessons as they engage in ongoing formative assessment of student progress. In this way, they focus on the language work necessary to make their classrooms equitable communities where *all* students can thrive.

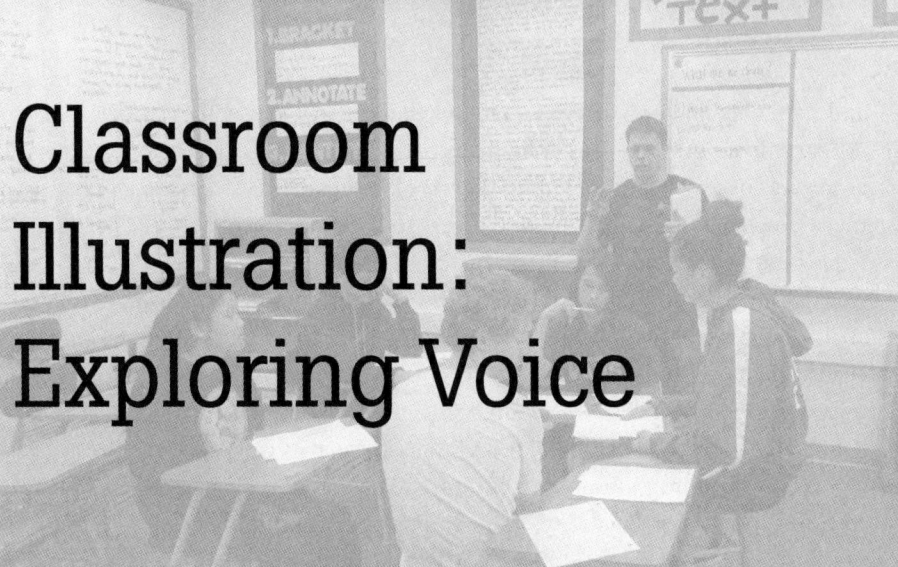

Classroom Illustration: Exploring Voice

*Our students need opportunities to think and to write and to write
deeply about things they care and are passionate about. Standards or no
standards, they need to find their voice—not just the style of their words
or their word choice—but the actual ideas behind them.*

—Gary

Meet Gary Miller, a sixth-grade teacher in a small rural school
district in northern California. Gary's class is considered
mainstream, although it includes a large number (seventeen
out of twenty-eight) of students from households where Span-
ish is the primary language. Many of his students are bilingual in Spanish and
English; they tested into a variety of English proficiency levels from beginner to
advanced on the California English Language Development Test (CELDT). In this
chapter, we illustrate how Gary engaged the whole class in a series of complex
text analysis activities and supported the English language learners' metalinguistic awareness through text analysis activities focused at the word, sentence,
and paragraph levels. Gary explores with his students how register, voice, and
the context of a discipline or discourse community can be reflected in word

choice and syntactical structures such as complex sentences and shifting pronouns. We see Gary's class focused not only on how texts work, but also more specifically on how language works in those texts through, for example, unpacking the language of texts to understand how word choice provides *register* or what he refers to as *voice* in a text.

In an effort to establish an equity-oriented classroom, Gary brought language into focus to support his English language learners' metalinguistic awareness through methods that inspired students to think about how language works. Table 4.1 is an overview of the lengthier unit of study on narrative writing that spanned approximately five weeks. Table 4.2 outlines Gary's approach to meeting the language objectives of the unit by identifying the language demands and designing language supports. We focus particularly on Gary's teaching of language at the lexicon (word) and grammar level. While his genre-based instructional design was similar to Rachel's (as described in Chapter 3), Gary's unit emphasized how authors made linguistic choices to show a specific purpose or express their individual voices.

Gary's language objectives included supporting his students in developing metalinguistic awareness—thinking about language use—by inviting them to focus on the language writers use to give the text *voice*, as well as the way writers craft texts with audience, purpose, and context in mind. Table 4.2 shows how Gary identified language demands in his unit plan at the levels we discussed in Chapter 2 and then designed targeted supports to give his students access and opportunities to learn the new language. His language supports at the lexicon and grammar level enabled them to talk about writers' choices at the discourse level.

As you'll see in the following pages, Gary's lesson sequence began with analysis of an unusual but real-world genre that gave students access to the concept of voice: greeting cards. Without pressure to follow complex plot lines, all his multilingual students were able to focus on the writers' choices of words and sentence structure for conveying particular messages. With a solid understanding of the concept, the students were then able to write and revise their own narrative texts for voice. The lessons illustrated in this chapter include:

1. Text Analysis: What Is Voice?
2. Using Voice as a Lens in Providing Peer Feedback
3. Revising for Voice

Table 4.1. Unit Overview: Text Analysis and Voice in Narrative Writing

What are the desired outcomes for my students?

Students' analyses of *voice* in various texts support them to write a reflective recount of an important event (real or imagined). Students explain how their analyses of texts impact their writing choices and process.

Common Core State Standard(s): Reading 1–10, Writing 3, 4–10

California ELD Standards—Interacting in Meaningful Ways, Learning about How English Works, Using Foundational Literacy Skills

Language Objectives—students learn and operationalize the academic language demands of reading, writing, listening, speaking, and analysis of a variety of texts. (See Table 4.2 for a magnified view of language demands, language objectives, and language supports.)
- Lexicon: descriptive vocabulary for writing and analyzing texts, e.g., active verbs, color words, sensory words, and vivid adjectives; metalanguage for talking about narrative texts, e.g., *plot, climax, conflict, chronological order, past, present, and future tenses,* and *theme*
- Grammar: compound and complex sentences; pronouns; prepositional phrases; adjective phrases
- Discourse: structures of narration, voice, sequencing, and time, including metalanguage for discourse patterns such as *planning, introducing, concluding.*

Students will know that:	Students will (do):
Authors make stylistic, organizational, language, and content choices based on purpose, audience, content, and context.	Read and interpret a variety of texts from different authors for a variety of audiences, contexts, and purposes
The analysis of various texts can support writing decisions.	Locate and explain how the text is crafted to express an author's intended goals
Writers use language to create voice, tone, and mood in narrative texts such as the reflective recount.	Use information from the analysis of texts to plan, draft, revise, and communicate students' own narrations
Narration and storytelling unfold in space and time; language choices are important to make story move effectively through time.	Use the language of the discipline to communicate a story effectively

How will I assess students along the way?

Formative Assessments	Summative Performance Tasks:
Voice investigation station handouts	Draft and revised writing
Short responses to text analysis questions (unpacking song lyrics)	Reflection on experiences
	Verbal explanations of thinking
Greeting card responses	
Daily reflections	**Other:**
Text-to-text analysis and planning (prewriting)	Running records
Early draft of reflective recount	Observation tools
TAG peer feedback conference sheets	Interview notes
Reflections on incorporating peer feedback	Recordings
	Portfolios

Table 4.2. Meeting Language Objectives: Identifying and Supporting Language Demands

Language Demands: Lexicon	Language Supports: Lexicon
Metalanguage for talking about narrative texts: • Voice • Narrative • Reflection • Recount • Message • Imagery • Descriptive/sensory language • Setting • Conflict • Complications • Plot • Climax • Character development • Dialogue • Theme • Active verbs • Figurative language: metaphor, simile, personification, etc. • Introduce • Conclude • Narrative techniques such as backstory, flashback, foreshadowing, and story-within-a-story *Sample language objective: identify points in a story where the author moves through time. Use the metalanguage terms* backstory, flashback, foreshadowing, *and* story-within-a-story.	Greeting card voice analysis Word wall with icons and visuals of content words and metalanguage Reference charts: lists of short phrases found often in whole-class and shared reading Word lists: active verbs, sensory words, color words, vivid adjectives, and functional language, e.g., *prewrite, draft, revise,* in a "tool kit" section of students' writer's notebooks Visuals on PowerPoint: graphics and icons to illustrate concepts Choral practice and repetition: words, phrases, and sentence starters. Digital photography: pictures of students engaged in each lesson used to lead students in reflective conversations about the literacy practices they had engaged in each day and to prompt discussion of time and space in storytelling and narration "My personal dictionary and thesaurus": students recorded new words, definitions, and picture clues in a notebook or log. Each student had his or her own log of words encountered during independent reading and in other tasks. Think-aloud process: using text and a document camera to demonstrate breaking down words, phrases, and punctuation and using context and other clues to determine word meanings. Read-aloud: modeling interest and active, fluid reading strategies, e.g., questioning the text, clarifying new words in context, and predicting
Language Demands: Grammar	**Language Supports: Grammar**
• Syntax: expanded noun phrases with prepositional, adjective, and adverbial and other modifiers in order to give more detailed imagery • Compound and complex sentences • Prepositional phrases • Adjective phrases • Nominalization • Pronoun usage *Sample language objectives: trace the use of pronouns in a section of text and explain their functions. Revise a plain sentence by adding vivid sensory details including adjectives, adverbs, and figurative language.*	Sentence comparison: Gary cut out various aspects of sentences and invited his students to compare sentences both with and without extended descriptors and modifiers. Think-aloud and read-aloud (modeling fluent reading): Using the document camera to highlight carefully selected sentences in a given text, Gary modeled his thought process and questioned each highlighted section, making notes about what each word in a sentence was doing and how it contributed to the meaning of that sentence and the text as a whole. Text compare/contrast activity: Gary wrote two pieces to show how informational texts often condense ideas through sentence combining, use of pronouns, and nominalization in order to create more precise and detailed sentences. Sentence unpacking: Students practice unpacking and creating compound and complex sentences during text analysis. Reference charts: class-developed resources for student reference posted on walls of classroom

Continued on next page

Table 4.2. Continued

Language Demands: Discourse	Language Supports: Discourse
Literary texts with varied time-order structures. Texts may: • Begin in the past and move to the present, • Be told entirely in the past tense, • Move from the present to the past and end discussing the future, or • Represent some other narrative structure. *Sample language objective: identify the author's use of verb tense, connectives, time order, and transition words. Explain the impact of these words on the text using the words* present, past, *and* future.	Targeted questions: specific, consistent, and clear questions to unpack each section of the texts, e.g., What is this part of the text *saying*? What is this [same] part of the text *doing*? Optional sentence frames for each answer to the questions. Document camera think-aloud: to highlight selected sentences in a given text and model thought process of analyzing text and answering questions about time order, verb tense, connectives, and transition language.

General Language Supports

Teacher models the processes of prewriting with think-aloud by using a graphic organizer under a document camera to show how brainstorming works—with student interaction and participation

Read-aloud: teacher reads the text aloud while students follow to model active reading strategies such as predicting, questioning the text, and clarifying words in context. Use of interaction, visuals, and realia maximizes comprehension.

Document camera, video clips, technology, and media show images of what drafting and revising might look like throughout the writing process.

Video analysis of peer feedback conferencing (TAG): **T**ell what you like, **A**sk thought-provoking questions, **G**ive suggestions

Group and partner work for collaboration and practice using academic language, including metalanguage to describe processes such as *drafting, revising,* and *explaining*

Checklists for formative assessment of students as they engaged in tasks and language development

Daily warm-ups, reviews, and reflections—engaging students in each of these activities with a variety of supports and independent practice

Exit tickets focused on a word or language function used each day

Setting the Stage for Interacting in Meaningful Ways

To build a collaborative writing community in their classrooms, the lesson study team designed student writing groups. In his class, Gary worked with students to select writing groups by giving each student the opportunity to choose the peers with whom they would like to work. He gave students the opportunity to name three peers and promised that they would get at least one of their choices. Gary then went through the students' lists and arranged groups, honoring requests as much as possible while balancing gender, skill, and language proficiency as well as social and behavioral concerns.

Once groups were set up in early September, Gary added various ongoing activities to strengthen students' understanding of collaboration. For example, in their writing groups students designed a team poster that displayed their collaboratively determined team name, logo, and slogan. (Each group also designed a team handshake!) On their posters, the teams wrote at least five group norms that they believed would be important to the group's functioning. These group norms included such things as "listen to each other," "don't interrupt," "be honest," and "stay on task." Gary laminated these posters and placed each one in a small metal stand so they stood upright in the center of tables when students worked in their writing groups. Every time students met as a group, they revisited the norms they had created, discussed them, and added to them if necessary. From this point on, Gary called the writing groups by their team names: the Writing Warriors, the Write Ones, the Dragon Writers, etc.

In a classroom with students whose English proficiency ranges as widely as in Gary's class, these types of established routines can be essential to supporting multilingual students' social and academic development. Whereas some students might be shy or embarrassed to share their writing with more English-fluent classmates they barely know, the ongoing writing groups allowed for a greater level of trust. Over time the students learned about one another's strengths and needs. ELLs came to trust that their group members were there to help them, not to make fun of them. Fluent English speakers learned that even if their ELL classmates didn't know as many words in English as they did, they still had active imaginations and could provide valuable feedback on their peers' ideas. In this way, Gary was able to increase the degree of equity for all students while remaining accountable for his ELLs' language learning.

In another ongoing practice, students in Gary's class used spiral-bound writer's notebooks each time there was a writing activity, as well as a separate notebook, called "my personal dictionary and thesaurus," to log new vocabulary. The writer's notebooks were separated into sections that included a "tool kit" in the back, which housed punctuation resources and a variety of word lists: transition words, active verbs, sensory adjectives, etc. The tool kit also contained a variety of other supports such as templates with sentence starter options for group discussions. These sentence starters prompted students to ask for their peers' opinions and suggested ways to disagree appropriately, to build on one another's work, and to ask clarifying questions. Gary checked the carefully organized writer's notebooks regularly so that when he asked students to turn to a specific page or tool, he knew they could immediately find it.

Initially there was a great degree of teacher direction in setting up what Gary called a "writing classroom," which, as the year progressed, moved toward a more student-driven format for peer response. For example, in their initial design of writing groups, Gary and the lesson study team used a structure called TAG. This acronym stands for *tell* something you like, *ask* a thought-provoking question, and *give* suggestions. When students began to respond to one another's writing, they used this structure and recorded their responses on handouts. This structure was designed to hold students accountable for participating and to provide teachers with a written product to assess. In each TAG conference, students took turns to tell something they liked, ask questions, and give suggestions to the writer. The writer could decide on his or her own how to incorporate the feedback into revisions. Gary gradually removed the TAG structure, so that toward the end of the year, his students were running their writing groups almost entirely independently.

The writing groups and writer's notebooks were particularly valuable in giving the multilingual students equitable (rather than just equal) access to learning opportunities. With the writer's notebooks, students could refer to resources as they needed them. Gary could direct the class to particular pages with sentence structures or vocabulary lists that they might use in their writing; ELLs could turn to the linguistic supports as often as they wanted and could add definitions, for example, in their home languages to help them learn new concepts and words. In keeping with GBI's emphasis on flexible approaches to text, Gary made sure that his students understood the tool kit as a resource they could use no matter what genre or text type they were reading or writing, rather than as separate, fixed formulas. The tools likewise supported students' language development by allowing them to experiment with language at multiple levels (lexical, grammatical, and discourse).

Classroom Snapshot 1

Text Analysis: What Is Voice?

Gary had observed Laura Zarano, his colleague in the lesson study, teach a multimodal lesson about voice that involved music, collaboration, and writing. To introduce his students to the notion of voice, Gary modeled his lesson after Laura's design by selecting various pieces of music that reflected different musical genres, lyrics, styles, tones, and moods. He played brief excerpts of each of the eight songs, and after listening to each excerpt, students wrote a short list of words for each song responding to a single question: what makes this song unique? Students wrote their lists on sticky notes for each song. Their lists included the styles of music (such as hip-hop, country, pop, and rock); the type of lyrics (such as rhyme and storytelling); and the emotional impact on the listener (such as sad, positive, inspirational, and funny).

Next, Gary wanted to push students further toward the notion of voice as not only *what* you say but also *how* you say it. This lesson began by reading lyrics from the song "Somewhere over the Rainbow" by E. Y. Harburg. Gary invited the students to listen to him as he read the song lyrics with no intonation or feeling whatsoever. Next he announced, "I'm going to play a short excerpt, or section, of this song from ten different renditions, or remixes, of the same song. I want you to listen carefully to each rendition. After each rendition, we'll stop and you'll make notes about how the song was sung. After you make notes, you'll talk in your writing groups, and then together we'll chart some ideas that we come up with together as a class for each rendition." (Some of the artists included Judy Garland, the Ramones, and Israel Kamakawiwoʻole.) After the students had taken notes and discussed each rendition of the song, Gary prompted them to list what was unique about each one. Here, the lists included words such as *formal, casual, upbeat, full of life, dead sounding, positive, peppy, quiet, soft, sad,* and *depressing.* Gary returned to the written lyrics and reminded his students, "All of these words that we charted for each rendition are different, aren't they? Ha! Isn't that interesting . . . because we wrote these words about the same lyrics! What makes each rendition different?" As Gary debriefed this question with his students, they came up with a definition of *voice* as not only what you say (the song lyrics) but also how you say it (the different musical renditions), as they had discovered in the last part of the task.

Next, Gary called attention to the various blank charts he had hung around the room, with titles of several of the texts the class had recently read together written at the top of each chart. In small groups, students were to make word lists on the charts responding to the question: how would you describe the voice in this text? Gary reminded students to refer to the words on the charts they had just created during the analysis of music renditions. Students brainstormed ideas in their small groups and then transferred their lists to the chart paper. Gary closed this lesson with a discussion that reviewed a shared understanding of voice as: what you say and how you say it; voice is what makes the writing unique.

In an effort to encourage metalinguistic awareness, Gary's next step was to have students focus specifically on the language writers use to give texts voice. Inspired by Rachel Easton's classroom and that of another lesson study colleague, Elizabeth Wright, Gary designed a voice investigation station lesson with both informational and narrative texts. He posted short texts around the classroom and provided a handout with questions (listed below) for each piece of writing. Students traveled around the room in their writing groups and read the piece of writing, discussed the questions, and wrote answers together.

Voice Questions for Investigation Stations

1. How would you describe the *voice* of this piece?
2. What specific *language* (words, sentences, and punctuation) gave the text voice?

3. Why do you think the writer chose this kind of voice for this text? (Think about the purpose, audience, context, and content of the text.)

The texts that Gary posted around the room were selected for their dramatically different register: from formal academic language to more conversational informal language. Some of the voices were dialectical, some used code-switching, and some reflected personality traits of a character in the text, the writer, or the narrator. The texts also differed in topic, content, intended audiences, and point of view.

In the group discussion that followed the voice investigation stations, Gary began with global debriefing questions about the experience. He asked, "Which pieces were the most enjoyable to read and why?"

Antonio responded, "I liked the ones that were written in a cool way, with the words I use with my friends."

Gary continued, "Why did you like these the best?"

Another student responded, "Because it sounds like they're talking to me and like they know me." Most of Gary's students said they enjoyed the texts that were written in casual voices and in first person and that described topics and events they cared about. When Gary asked why, some of the responses included "passionate," "seemed real," "emotional," and "dramatic."

Gary then asked his students, "How do you know that the authors were passionate, emotional, or dramatic?" The students responded with a list of specific words in the texts that added imagery, such as *harsh, over the moon, bloody wreck*, and *hot mess*. They also noticed how punctuation such as all capital letters, exclamation points, and ellipsis added to the voice of some of the texts. Gary's students commented that the excerpts from legal briefs, textbooks, and technical directions for setting up a DVD player were *boring, formal, professional*, and *hard to understand*. The list of words students provided to explain why they thought these texts were boring included *nuclear, parliament, undertook, reign, whereas, sequentially*, and *non-linear*.

Gary supported his students' efforts to stretch their vocabulary by discussing how some of the language used in the texts the students liked included words they use frequently in their discourse communities at home and with their friends at school. He explained the metalanguage term *register* by projecting an image of two kids walking together and talking and asked students what kind of register the kids were most likely using. The students responded with words such as *everyday language, slang*, and *"normal" speech*. When discussing the less preferred informational texts, they suggested that the register was "bossy, smart language." Gary created a register T-chart with two columns—one titled Informal and the other Formal. His students went back to the texts from the investigation stations and selected words and phrases to go in each of the register columns (see Figure 4.1).

Informal Language	Formal Language
harsh	nuclear
over the moon	parliament
bloody wreck	undertook
hot mess	reign
	whereas
	sequentially
	nonlinear

Figure 4.1. Register T-chart.

Gary explained to his students that *register* is an academic vocabulary term for *voice*, and his students marveled at the humor: *register* is *voice* in a formal *register*. And with that, they decided to continue to use the term *voice* because it fit the context of their classroom. Giving students the choice of metalanguage terminology fits with the core concept of SFL that language be discussed functionally rather than prescriptively. It doesn't matter what term the class uses to talk about the role of word choice in register so long as the students understand what it means, how to see it in other writers' texts, and how to use it in their own.

The opportunity to compare and contrast language use across a variety of texts allowed Gary to engage students in further unpacking syntactical structures. He extracted several excerpts from the investigation station texts and led students through an interactive process of sentence combining. He also used these text analysis activities as an opportunity to investigate how authors use reference devices (e.g., pronouns, demonstratives, and synonym substitutions) to create cohesive texts that successively add new information (Brisk, 2015; de Oliveira & Schleppegrell, 2015). For example, Gary selected an excerpt from a text about honeybees. Through his laptop, he projected the paragraph onto the screen and invited his students to look at how the subject of a particular sentence changes throughout the course of the paragraph. "Let's take the first sentence." Gary highlighted the sentence and read it aloud, "'Honeybees are nature's gifts and must be protected.' What is the subject of this sentence? What is this sentence about?"

"Honeybees."

"Right," Gary answered, "and what about honeybees?"

Several students called out, "They must be protected."

Gary pushed the class, "Look how the next sentence begins: 'These sweet tiny friends . . .' What are the sweet tiny friends?"

"Honeybees."

"Yes, and look at a later sentence in that paragraph: 'They make honey for all of us to enjoy.' Who are *they*?"

Most of the class shouted, "The honeybees!"

"Right," Gary confirmed, "so what happened from *honeybees* to *these sweet tiny friends* to *they*?"

A few students suggested that the name changed to pronouns.

Gary accepted their response and probed further, "Yes—why do you think that is?"

A more candid student spoke for the class, "I don't know."

Gary directed the students' focus to the text on the document camera and asked, "How would it sound if the author wrote *honeybees* in every sentence?" He read the paragraph out loud and replaced *honeybees* every time there was a pronoun or metaphor for honeybees.

The students laughed. "That sounds crazy!"

"Exactly," Gary agreed. "Authors use pronouns to refer to something or someone that they have already introduced. They may do this for a variety of reasons, but one reason—as you all pointed out—is that it sounds repetitive to keep using the proper names over and over again."

Gary used these text analysis activities as an opportunity to show students some of the ways that language is used differently in narrative and in informational writing. He had selected both informational and narrative texts carefully so that some of the differences would stand out. By the end of this series of lessons, Gary and his students had tackled a variety of new ideas about how language is used across contexts and disciplines.

While these processes benefit all students, ELLs who are just learning to distinguish between formal and informal registers are especially in need of the explicit attention Gary brought to how authors choose words for particular purposes. Students who have not grown up hearing these varieties of English are less likely to be able to articulate why they are different or to know how to deploy the linguistic resources needed to establish voice in their own writing (Ramanathan & Atkinson, 1999). Gary's next lesson helped his students transition from identifying voice to representing their own voices through writing.

Classroom Snapshot 2

Using Voice as a Lens in Providing Peer Feedback

Just before the events of the following snapshot, Gary's students had written their first draft of a reflective recount of an important event (imagined or real). The draft was written for an audience and context of their choosing. The following task was designed for students to give one another feedback about whether the voice was appropriate and effective for the selected audience and context as well as the story they chose to tell.

Gary began the lesson by reminding his students, "We've been talking about the word *voice*. Use your voices and shout out the word: VOICE!"

The students shouted "VOICE!" together.

Gary continued, "What is voice?"

The students read aloud from a PowerPoint slide projected at the front of the room, "Voice is: What you say and how you say it, your formal or informal *register*, the tone in your words, the feeling of your ideas, speaking with actions, the freedom to use your voice to express your feelings."

Following these reminders, Gary distributed a worksheet that was titled: "Voice is: *What* you say and *How* you say it." He then solicited another round of call and response by asking, "Guys, shout out: what is voice?"

The boys responded, "Voice is: *What* you say and *How* you say it!" Then Gary repeated the call and response technique with the girls. These practices were clearly engaging his students, who appeared to be focused and eagerly awaiting their next task.

Next, Gary explained to the class that they would begin with a review to make sure everyone was prepared to give one another feedback on the voice in their writing. "Let's look at greeting cards to talk about voice." On his PowerPoint slide, he showed a greeting card labeled Card 1. This was a get-well card that featured cartoons and was clearly intended for a child. He asked students, "*What* is this card saying? And *how* is this card saying it?" Then he asked the same two questions for Card 2, which was a humorous get-well card intended for an adult. Gary directed these same two questions to Card 3, which was a serious get-well card with a heartfelt message.

Through this activity, Gary engaged his students in thinking about *content*, *purpose*, *audience*, and *context* as they related to voice. For example, he facilitated a whole-class discussion about why they thought the serious get-well card would be appropriate in certain situations where the humorous ones would not. In this way, students were able to analyze content, context, purpose, audience, and voice in a familiar, accessible text—greeting cards. Gary reminded his students, "In the second card, the *what* was to get well; the *how* was with humor." He asked them to think about the context of this type of card. "What type of *situation* is appropriate for sending this card? To whom would it be appropriate to send the card and for what purposes?" Students thought the recipient's illness or injury would likely have been temporary so the card would be appropriate for someone who would most likely recover soon.

Gary projected an image of the next card on the screen. "In this card, the *what* was also to get well, but in this card, the *how* was peaceful, serious, and heartfelt. When you think about voice, you have to think about the audience. You have to ask, who will get the card? What kinds of health issues are likely to prompt sending this card?" Gary continued to elicit ideas from students about why the voice of each card was appropriate for certain purposes, contexts, and audiences.

In the next part of the lesson, Gary told the students they would be looking at another set of greeting cards in their writing groups. Students cheered loudly; they were clearly enthusiastic about this activity. Gary showed a PowerPoint slide with a Mother's Day card that had a picture of Snoopy on it. He asked his students to write on their handout the *what* and the *how* of the card's message. One group wrote, "What: have a good mother's day. How: with hugs from Snoopy, with love." The next card was a more serious card. A group wrote, "The *what* is the same—but the *how* is different."

Gary debriefed this activity by saying, "Thumbs up if you think the message is the same but it sounds completely different!" Students all put their thumbs in the air. Gary continued, "It's more serious. What's making it more serious?"

Students responded, "The pictures . . . the words . . . There are more words. . . . It seems like it's from an adult to an older mother. . . . It has bigger words. . . . The words are in cursive. . . . It's more *formal*."

Gary closed this activity by asking, "What is the *what* of all three of these cards?"

His students responded, "Mother's Day, to have a good one."

Gary reviewed with the class, "The first card, Snoopy, how does the writer say it? What voice does he use?" He paused as the students talked briefly with one another. "Humorous, but happy at the same time, right? Card 2 was calming. The register was more *formal*, and Card 3 was humorous, more so than the Snoopy card, joking around. The register was *informal*. A writer, simply by the words they use and the way they put those words together, can say the same thing (the *what*) in very different ways (the *how*) and to very different people in different situations, or *contexts*. The reasons greeting card designers do this is because they make cards for different purposes and different audiences. They want to make a card for everyone so they can make what?" He paused again, and the students joined him to shout, "MONEY!"

At this point in the lesson, Gary segued into his discussion of voice in the students' writing. He asked, "How many of you think you have used words to convey an appropriate voice in your writing according to the audience you're writing to? Thumbs up or down."

Students responded with mostly thumbs up, though several gave thumbs down.

Gary continued, "How many of you think you've used words to convey an appropriate voice in your writing according to the content, what you are writing about? Thumbs up or down."

Students responded with mostly thumbs up, but again, several thumbs faced down.

Finally, Gary asked, "How many of you think you've used words to convey an appropriate voice in your writing according to the purpose, or the reason that you are writing? Thumbs up or down."

Just as before, the students responded primarily with thumbs up.

Before he set them to the task of sharing their writing with their peers and receiving feedback from each other, Gary reminded students of the ways in which voice would be different across each of their texts. He referred them to the reference charts around the room to use when they engaged in peer feedback. The charts included lists of words showing emotion, descriptive language, strong verbs, academic vocabulary, and discipline-specific vocabulary. Gary had created each of these charts with his students, but there are also many resources for charts like these available to teachers free online.

Gary continued the lesson by projecting another PowerPoint slide that asked, "Is there voice in our writing?" He then projected an excerpt from a published text, selected a student volunteer to read the excerpt, and asked the students to turn and tell their partners *what* this author was saying. He paused to give them time to turn and talk. They then shared out, and Gary wrote on the board, "The text says that ancient Athens wasn't a democracy."

He then turned to the class, "Now, turn and tell your partner *how* this author is saying it," pausing to give them time to turn and talk to their partners. When they shared out, Gary wrote on the board, "*How* they are saying it: with a list of facts."

Gary showed another sample that made the same argument but that used an anecdote of a personal experience as an analogy. He again elicited responses from his students about the nature of these differences. A student responded, "In the first one, she just lists some facts. The second one is like a story. I think they're both good explanations, but they do it differently."

Focusing on the boy's comment about making a strong argument by telling a story, Gary asked him, "Billy, is there a place where she does that well?"

Billy walked to the screen and pointed, "Right here when she says, 'that isn't very democratic or just.' She uses great words when she does that, like *democratic* and some other words like *just*."

Several other students pointed out words they had found that strengthened the author's argument, including *undoubtedly* and *unfortunately*. One explained, "All of those big words kind of give her a strong voice."

Gary concluded, "So, you've decided that the piece on the right has a very different voice even though the *what* is the same."

Students seemed to agree, so Gary announced, "Now you're going to do this in your writing groups. You all have selected a voice that fits your audience and purpose, and in your writing groups you're going to respond to each other's writing and talk to each other about the voice you hear. We'll do this again after you write another piece in a different voice and then one more time to compare between the two pieces. Are you ready?"

"Yes!"

Gary reminded his students about some of their writing group procedural norms, which he had projected on a PowerPoint slide at the front of the room. "You are either the reader or the listener. Remember to TAG. Repeat after me." The students echoed him as he called out the letters of the mnemonic: "T is for **T**ell something you like. A is for **A**sk questions. G is for **G**ive suggestions." At that point, the students moved into their writing groups.

In Gary's class, students were assigned jobs in their writing groups. The secretaries picked up the table signs and folders and distributed the folders to their peers. When they returned to their seats, Gary asked the timekeepers from each table to pick out their favorite norm from the slide, read the norm, and explain why the norm was important. Gary wanted to briefly reinforce the importance of students following the peer feedback norms they themselves had created weeks before.

The students were engaged. They stayed on task; they were cooperative and followed each of the TAG steps. They wrote feedback on sticky notes, and the writer receiving the feedback attached the notes to his or her handout in columns for TAG (see Figure 4.2). As Gary floated around the room to support and record notes, he noticed that each of the three students in one group, the Writing Warriors, had provided at least one suggestion and compliment to each member of the group but seemed to have trouble asking questions about one another's writing. Pointing to a reference chart listing possible thought-provoking TAG questions (What are you writing about? What is your purpose for writing this? Who is your audience? How do you want the reader to feel when they read your writing?), Gary reminded the group that these are the types of questions to ask when they get stuck and can't think of what to ask. He made a note to revisit the question-asking piece of the process the next day.

In the writing groups in Gary's class, the students have built mini-cultures, developing their own group norms and practices. The TAG process for peer feedback imposes a loose structure of questions but otherwise leaves the focus of response up to readers and writers. In what ways have you used peer feedback in your classes? What supports did you provide to guide students? Where have your students struggled to provide appropriate or useful feedback to their peers?

Tell something you like:	Ask questions:	Give Suggestions:

Figure 4.2. TAG handout.

Classroom Snapshot 3

Revising for Voice

In his extended lesson plan, updated based on the information he had gleaned from assessing his students informally the day before, Gary used a document camera to project a piece of his own writing on the topic of bike safety and helmet laws. He had prepared two pieces of writing in different genres (one narrating and one explaining) using different voices, writing to different audiences in different contexts. Additionally, he included several obvious and several more subtle flaws in his writing in order to guide students toward understanding how descriptive and figurative language can impact the overall meaning of a text.

Gary began by reading his first piece (the informational text) aloud and asked his students for feedback. He reminded them to ask him first who the audience was and what his purposes were in writing the piece. He projected his essay with a document camera so students could see how he interacted with his text. Students suggested that the piece was written for a local newspaper as a letter to the editor to explain to the community why bike helmet laws should be enforced. They labeled the voice "formal, educational, and serious." Next, the students provided feedback on Gary's writing, discussing it thoroughly as they went through each point. They followed the same process for Gary's narrative piece on the same topic. Gary had written this piece as an imagined reflective recount of a head injury he had sustained while riding without a helmet. Students felt that the purpose was the same, to convince people to wear helmets, but they highlighted aspects of differences in the way the piece was structured. Finally, the class provided feedback on ways to improve the piece. After the lesson, Gary revised both texts based on his students' comments and suggestions.

The next day, Gary brought his first drafts and his revised texts to school and projected them one at a time under the document camera. He modeled his own process of reflection and shared the differences in his writing based on the students' suggestions, thinking aloud about each of the choices he had made as he revised. As he went along, he underlined the revisions and explained why he had added, changed, or deleted each part. He identified the individual students who had made those suggestions and thanked them. He pointed to the reference charts and drew attention to the sentences he had combined and changes he had made in nominalization, punctuation, and descriptive and figurative language.

Before he finished, Gary revisited the "**A**sk questions" aspect of the TAG, explaining to his students that it was their questions that made his pieces stronger. He went back and forth from the questions he had written down to the revisions he had made in his writing because of their questions. Some of the questions were as follows:

- Why did you choose this topic?
- What did [an object or person] look like?
- How does [a word or phrase] specifically show your voice?
- What words did you use that you think reflected your voice the best?
- Can you turn that verb or adjective into a noun?
- How about using a pronoun there?
- Why don't you try combining these two sentences?

This aspect of the lesson concluded with Gary explaining how each question encouraged him to choose an appropriate or effective voice (the *how*) to present information (the *what*) to a specific audience depending on the specific purposes. Gary and his students added these questions to the reference chart with the list of TAG questions. This chart served as a resource during the next TAG conferences.

Gary closed the day's activities by explaining to his students that their work over the next week in class would be to revise their reflective recounts based on peers' suggestions, just as he had revised his writing based on the students' suggestions.

Reflecting on Genre-Based Instruction for Equity

Gary's lessons focused on developing a metalinguistic awareness that language is used in a variety of ways for a variety of purposes. After the activities depicted in these snapshots, Gary invited his students to take another look at their reflective recounts and write informational texts on the same or a related topic. This way, they could make the kinds of language choices that he had made when he modeled his two different pieces of writing, a reflective recount of a bike accident and an editorial on bike safety. Gary's approach to language-focused, genre-based instruction is far from formulaic. He regularly engaged his students in critical thinking about a variety of rhetorical, stylistic, and organizational moves that writers make in texts for a variety of purposes, audiences, and contexts. This approach is GBI at its best. The music and greeting card analysis activities introduced students to the idea that within any given genre, texts may have certain stable features, but they vary in other ways depending on the author's purpose, intended audience, content, and context. While developing this fundamental understanding, the class also collaboratively developed a shared metalanguage that they later used to talk about their own writing.

Gary's approach, like Rachel's in Chapter 3 and Talia's in the next chapter, is based on the notion that equity teaching means *all* students receive challenging and engaging literacy instruction, especially English language learners for whom instruction is too often rote and formulaic. Rachel, Gary, and Talia's views are consistent with the research that frames equity teaching as providing access to high-quality educational experiences. We provide recommendations in the appendix on page 149 for additional approaches to planning, teaching, and assessing language-focused lessons in equitable ways.

Claude Goldenberg and Rhoda Coleman's (2010) synthesis of more than twenty years of research suggests that the foundation of an effective literacy program for English language learners is similar to that of an effective literacy program for fluent English speakers. High-quality instruction targets complex sets of skills and concepts and should be taught explicitly and with interactive methods that challenge students both cognitively and linguistically. However, English language learners must be provided language supports in order to access grade-level literacy practices and learn academic content and skills. The snapshots in Chapters 3 and 4 illustrate several research-based language supports, including a focus on academic vocabulary use in meaningful contexts, a focus on text and language structures, well-designed opportunities for oral language production, and additional practice and repetition (Goldenberg & Coleman, 2010). In Chapter 5, we see how Talia used information from her ongoing formative assessment of her students' learning to inform her practices.

Classroom Illustration: Formative Assessment

My kids are falling in love with writing groups. I am noticing they are
saying things like "we get to write" instead of "we have to write."

—Talia

I n the last two chapters, Rachel Easton and Gary Miller introduced us to a variety of text analysis activities situated in genre-based instruction as a way to focus on the language of texts and to encourage metalinguistic awareness for their English language learners. Talia Fenton, whom you'll meet in this chapter, also uses a process of close reading and text analysis to promote language and literacy development. However, as we immerse you in Talia's teaching, we do so through a different lens, one that focuses on how she uses formative assessment to inform instruction, demonstrating a central form of accountability to multilingual students.

This chapter focuses on the formative assessment techniques that Talia embedded in text analysis and student collaborative learning activities as her eighth-grade English language learners engaged in reading and responding to culturally diverse texts. Like those depicted in the preceding chapters, Talia's classroom practices also reflect a language-focused, flexible approach to genre-based instruction as she supports her students in investigating how authors integrate evidence from sources into the texts they produce. Although the students were working on text analysis activities similar to those illustrated in Rachel's classroom, the purpose of this chapter is to illustrate the various ways that Talia used information from her focused daily formative assessment of students to inform her instruction. These assessments allowed Talia to maintain her accountability to her students' learning needs by designing a series of supports and extensions to promote reading, writing, and revision.

The overarching unit of study described in this chapter was centered on reading and responding to multicultural texts. Beyond inspiring this group of multilingual students with rich literary experiences, Talia sought to prepare students for reading and responding to literature both in classroom-embedded assessments and on standardized tests, which often include response to literature tasks. To respond both orally and in writing about the themes from literature, students must comprehend and extend their thinking about the themes.

Talia's lessons in this unit were designed to help students actively read and consider a variety of issues in the literature so that they could draw ideas for their own writing. Throughout the reading process, students stopped at key places in the texts and responded to prompts for discussion. They took notes in a section of their writer's notebooks called a "data bank" that soon became packed with data (purposeful and organized notes) from their reading. The goal was to make the reading process so productive that by the time students finished the reading, much of the writing was already done. Table 5.1 provides an overview of the genre-based focus, responding to literature and writing reviews. This unit of study took approximately six weeks and focused on the theme of multicultural voices in literature. Table 5.2 then provides an overview of the language-focused approach Talia took in designing lessons in the unit of study.

In this chapter, we see how Talia used formative assessment to inform her planning. Her initial focus for this unit was to guide her English language learners to understand and operationalize the language needed for writing responses to literature in a structured five-paragraph, school-based writing task, but careful attention to her students' learning guided her to modify her instruction toward a real-life writing task, writing reviews, which could follow a more flexible structure. In both of these tasks, the lexicon-level emphasis in her lessons helps ELLs get repeated exposure to academic vocabulary they might otherwise not hear very often. They see the metalanguage recycled throughout lessons that both talk about the concepts and support students' using them in their own writing. As much research has shown, English language learners enter school (in any grade) with considerably smaller vocabulary knowledge then their English-fluent peers, putting them at a disadvantage for both grade-level reading and writing (Hinkel, 2015). Talia's

Table 5.1. Unit Overview: Writing Reviews and Responding to Multicultural Literature

What are the desired outcomes for my students?

Students' close reading of literary (and other) texts supports them in responding to literature and writing reviews. Students explain how they drew evidence from texts and other sources to support their writing.

Common Core State Standard(s): Reading 1–10, Writing 1, 2, 4–10

California ELD Standards—Interacting in Meaningful Ways, Learning about How English Works, Using Foundational Literacy Skills

Language Objectives—students learn and operationalize the academic language demands of reading, writing, listening, and speaking about literature, responding to prompts about multicultural literature, and writing reviews. (See Table 5.2 for a magnified view of language demands, language objectives, and language supports.)
- Lexicon: culturally and historically situated vocabulary; metalanguage for talking and writing about the cultural and historical background of authors and texts; metalanguage for explaining, recommending, or critiquing products, movies, books, music, etc.
- Grammar: clarity and cohesion in sentence structure
- Discourse: structure of texts; register differences in responding to prompts about literature and written reviews

Students will know that:	Students will (do):
Close and analytic reading of literary texts supports comprehension.	Read and interpret a text for literary elements, devices, and themes.
Drawing evidence from the text supports written responses to literature.	Keep a "data bank" where students collect quotes, excerpts, words, and phrases from the texts they are reading that may be integrated later into longer pieces of writing.
(Multicultural) literature is written in historical, cultural, social, and political contexts.	Locate and explain the historical, cultural, social, and political contexts at play in the text.
Comprehension includes understanding the influences and implications of a text both in its own time and throughout time.	Analyze how texts are crafted to express an author's intended goals.
Authors make stylistic, organizational, language, and content choices based on topic, content, thematic purposes, other literary purposes, audience, and context.	Use information from the analysis of a variety of texts to plan, draft, revise, and communicate written responses to prompts about the literature and write reviews.
Writing responses to prompts about literature requires abstract text interpretations and drawing evidence from texts.	Use the metalanguage of the discipline (*plot, theme, characters' motivation, symbolism, imagery, metaphor*, etc.) and general academic language, e.g., *interpret, compare, develop*, to communicate analytical thinking both orally and in writing.
Writing reviews requires analysis, comparisons, attention to detail, descriptions, personal experience, and authenticity.	Write a review: create an original thesis based on a product, movie, book, or other subject of a review. Use examples and comparisons to support the thesis, concluding with a strong recommendation or criticism.

How will I assess students along the way?

Formative Assessments	Summative Performance Tasks:
Read-around, small-group read-aloud running check	Drafts with revised written responses to literature
Short oral and written responses to literature	Drafts with revised written reviews
Observations during investigation stations	Reflections on experiences
Handouts with text analysis responses	Verbal explanations of thinking
Annotation of texts—active reading	
Short responses to texts-analysis questions	**Other:**
Daily reflections—short responses to literature	Running records
Text-to-text analysis—planning handouts/ graphic organizers/data bank	Observation tools
	Interview notes
Early drafts	Recordings
TAG peer feedback conference sheets	Portfolios
Reflections on incorporating feedback with highlighting	

Table 5.2. Meeting Language Objectives: Identifying and Supporting Language Demands

Language Demands: Lexicon	**Language Supports: Lexicon**
Metalanguage for talking about historical and cultural background of authors and texts: • Context • Social context • Political context • Historical context • Cultural context • Influence • Background of an author • Personal experience • Economic • Class • Culture, ethnicity, religion • Dialect Metalanguage for talking about literary texts: • Theme • Plot • Setting • Character development • Motivation • Figurative language • Idiomatic language • Time and story sequencing • Text structure Culturally and historically situated vocabulary words and idioms used in selected short stories Figurative language *Sample language objective: identify and explain an idiom or metaphor using one or more of these terms:* comparison, hyperbole, imagery, *or* impact.	Word wall: lists of frequently used metalanguage and other academic vocabulary Word lists: kept in a "tool kit" section of students' writer's notebooks Visuals (graphics and icons) for each word Choral practice and repetition: students say key words and phrases aloud Digital photography: Talia took pictures of students as they engaged in each lesson and used the pictures to lead students in reflective conversations each day. Audio recording was also used when appropriate. Exit tickets: focused on a word used each day Model language analysis: Document camera used to highlight areas where texts used figurative language and idioms; class discussion of contributions of figurative language and idioms Video of teachers (directed and filmed by Talia) engaging in academic discussions about literature Image analysis of figurative language, figures of speech, and idioms (e.g., "when pigs fly") to illustrate exaggeration and the relationships between the idioms and what they are referencing in the text
Language Demands: Grammar	**Language Supports: Grammar**
Clarity and cohesion in sentence structure through clear subjects, predicates, and modifiers Introduce examples with connectives to create cohesion: *for example, for instance, according to the text, nevertheless,* etc. *Sample language objective: use signal words such as* one reason, in addition, *or* finally *to introduce and integrate evidence, examples, or reasons into writing.*	Model sentence analysis: document camera for unpacking complex sentences and paragraphs. Interactive lesson using think-aloud and class discussion about sentence structure and word choices in the texts. "Try it" activity: cut up sentences to arrange and rearrange by using cohesive connectives; class discussions of the difference made by the use of signal/transition words.

Continued on next page

Table 5.2. Continued

Language Demands: Discourse	Language Supports: Discourse
How texts are organized, how each part of the text contributes to the whole, and why the author made the choices that he or she made	Read-aloud to model text analysis: use the document camera to highlight sections of text, model the process for annotating each section, make notes about what each part of the text was saying and doing, and identify how each part of the text contributed to the whole.
Differences in register between response to prompts about literature and written reviews depending on context, purpose, content, and intended audience	
Themes in literature are not typically stated outright or explicit.	Focus questions: specific, consistent, and clear targeted questions to unpack each section of the text. For example: What is this section of the text *saying*? What is this same section of the text *doing*?
Sample language objective: contrast the difference in register between two texts by identifying distinguishing words and phrases such as code-switching, *use of dialect, or conversational language.*	Sentence frames (as an option)
	Use of video to analyze the interactions of others engaged in discussion of literary texts
	Analysis of register in published reviews of books, movies, and video games written for different audiences
	Comparison lists of informal and formal register found online and/or created with students

General Language Supports

Audio recordings of authors reading their work

Read-aloud for modeling interest, prosody, and active reading strategies, e.g., questioning the text, clarifying new words in context, summarizing, and predicting

Teacher think-aloud and modeling note taking, annotating, and questioning during the active reading of literature

Think-aloud process for prewriting, drafting, and revising, as well as reflecting on how to incorporate peer feedback

Guided, collaborative, and independent practice reading, writing, summarizing themes, and discussing literature

Charts and posters for students to practice informal writing during the investigation stations

Handouts for the investigation stations with each question clearly written and room for responses. Each handout had sentence frames on the back as an option but not a requirement.

Use of video and photos for students to analyze the interactions of others and reflect on their work

Group and partner work for collaboration and practice using academic language

Checklists for formative assessment of students as they engaged in tasks and language development

Daily warm-ups, reviews, and reflections

Exit tickets focused on a word or language function used each day

Practice and scaffolding the use of sentence frames and terms language objectives (in Table 5.2) were therefore heavily focused on helping her ELL students catch up to their peers' lexical knowledge while learning the new vocabulary through the context of authentic texts that prepared them for writing on high-stakes assessments. Talia's lessons included a focus on the language students needed to use before, during, and after reading a text and the metalanguage for *interpreting*, *discussing*, *comparing*, and *critiquing* texts and the historical and social contexts in which the texts were written.

As you'll see in this chapter, Talia's lesson planning began by taking a more formulaic approach to supporting her students' academic writing process. She knew she would have to teach her multilingual students how to write essays specifically for high-stakes exams, so she started the writing part of the unit with a text structure that had no real-world counterpart. Through formative assessment that allowed her to monitor her students' learning throughout the unit, however, she realized that the assessment-focused text structure was restricting her students' ability to write independently. In the spirit of GBI, Talia sought out texts that represented the real-world functions of response to literature and shifted the class focus to analyzing and writing book, product, music, and movie reviews. The snapshots we see from Talia's unit covered the following lessons:

1. Setting Up for Formative Assessment
2. Literary Analysis
3. Experimenting with a Writing Formula: "The Full Meal Deal"
4. Text Analysis: Moving Away from Formulaic Writing Instruction
5. Peer Feedback and Revision

Talia's Classroom: Background

Talia believed that response to multicultural literature should begin by engaging students in active reading and interactive discussions of both the literature and its historical and cultural contexts. She wanted to engage her beginning and early intermediate ELL students in higher-level thinking about literature and related themes and issues. Her approach reflects Robert Probst's argument that "our primary goal in the English curriculum is not to make literary scholars of all of our students It is to make them readers and writers, independent and self-reliant thinkers who employ language and literature to enrich their lives" (1994, p. 44). Talia designed her lessons to include targeted stopping points so her students could talk and write about connections between the text, the contexts, the author's background, and their own thoughts and experiences. Students recorded notes, wrote annotations, and contributed to their writer's notebooks in what Talia called a "data bank." The data banks included short excerpts, quotations, and responses to questions about the reading. While this way of approaching literature instruction is key for all students, it's especially important for multilingual students. With multiple access points to the concepts, ELLs can build comprehension and deeper understanding and learn literacy strategies they will use throughout high school and college. Though they may not know as many words as their English-fluent peers, even as young teenagers multilingual students are able to draw on their wide-ranging life experiences to bring alternative interpretations to the discussion. Through oral discussion of reading texts, ELLs can highlight their own assets that their English-dominant classmates may not have.

English language learners, however, may still struggle to understand the linguistic aspects of multicultural texts. Through a supported and rigorous process of text analysis, Talia, like Rachel Easton and Gary Miller, provided opportunities for her ELLs to unpack how texts work. There is a clear emphasis on rigor in the Common Core State Standards for the English language arts. Rather than viewing rigor as simply an increase in text complexity, however, we interpret it in the way suggested by literacy scholars Kylene Beers and Robert Probst: "Rigor is not an attribute of a text, but rather a characteristic of our behavior with that text. Put another way, rigor resides in the energy and attention given *to* the text, not in the text itself" (2013, p. 21). This attention to text can be especially beneficial for ELLs, who have a harder time making meaning from complex texts due to their limited familiarity with the ways language is used in academic writing. Explicit instruction in how to read for various purposes and how to take notes gives multilingual students access to grade-level content and, therefore, rigor.

Talia planned ways to engage students in a variety of thoughtful interpretations of both the texts themselves and the historical, cultural, social, and political contexts in which the texts were conceived and developed. She chose two short stories from diverse authors that she felt would be age appropriate and could provide entry points for discussing the historical and cultural significance of literature. She understood that the integration of content from underrepresented voices in the literary canon is one dimension of multiculturalism and can be transformative for student learning (Banks & Banks, 1995). This chapter highlights the class's discussions of the short story "Thank you, M'am" by Langston Hughes and "My Name," an excerpt from *The House on Mango Street* by Sandra Cisneros. Talia planned to discuss Langston Hughes's contribution to the Harlem Renaissance and engage her students in thinking about how historical and cultural contexts influenced this author's writing. She chose the excerpt from *The House on Mango Street* because she hoped the story could facilitate a dialogue about names, heritage, gender expectations, and oral tradition. Talia believed that historical and cultural contexts were critical for identifying theme in both stories. She established teaching objectives to include active engagement with texts, class discussion, a focus on themes from the text, and connecting themes to cultural and historical contexts. These texts also allowed English language learners to draw on their background knowledge, including their own experiences moving between cultures and being unfamiliar with cultural ways of acting. Having some schema made accessing the plot and themes of the stories easier for students who were still working on decoding the language. The unit was rigorous because students interacted with accessible, high-interest literature and "explore[d] deeply and thoughtfully [the text's] subtleties and implications" (Beers & Probst, 2013, p. 21).

Classroom Snapshot 1

Setting Up for Formative Assessment

From the early planning stages of her unit on response to literature, Talia anticipated the culminating task for the unit: a written response to literature focused on the connections between the themes of the stories and the contexts in which the themes were conceived and produced. She understood that the traditional five-paragraph literary analysis essay was a school-based academic writing product that did not exist outside of academia, an issue that was confirmed when she tried to find authentic texts from real-world writing about various elements of literature, including prose, poetry, and drama. She recognized that a lack of real-world connections meant this particular form of essay challenged the spirit of genre-based instruction, but she also knew that her students would benefit both in school and in on-demand standardized assessment situations by learning to respond to prompts about themes in literature in a structured essay format.

In our work with teachers, we often discuss how some of the problems in students' writing result from lack of comprehension and analysis during their reading. Talia's lesson plans focused on comprehending and interpreting literature by writing throughout the reading process. She wanted to make sure that when it came time to write, students would have already located and considered the significance of evidence from the texts. This way, the writing practice would be more about organizing thoughts and notes and less about trying to remember what happened in the texts they had read.

In the spirit of backwards planning, Talia selected the central outcomes for her students' reading and writing and wrote a writing assessment prompt aligned with those goals. She knew where she wanted her students to go and therefore knew where to stop during the reading in order to support her students as they added to their notes and data banks about the texts. Talia engaged her English language learners in rigorous reading and writing experiences with language supports and high-interest accessible texts. She began the unit by displaying the final essay writing prompt and expectations on a poster in front of the room and unpacking the components of the prompt with her students so they understood what they would be expected to do during in reading, listening, speaking, and writing.

Talia's poster explained the following:

By the end of the unit, your writing will include:

1. A clear and focused response to the prompt in the form of an appropriate thesis statement, opinion, or claim about a theme from the literary text

2. Well-integrated evidence from the text to support your claim through quotations, excerpts, and examples woven smoothly into your writing

3. Explanations that connect the author's personal experience and the historical context of the text to the themes and the examples that you selected

With these criteria in mind, Talia gave her students the following writing task:

Select one of the texts we have read in our Voices from Multicultural Literature unit.

- Describe one of the themes from the piece you selected.

- Provide one or more examples from your data bank to illustrate the theme you described.

- Explain how the author's background and historical context are connected to the theme and the examples you chose.

- Use your data bank and the anchor charts and other resources in the classroom.

With this emphasis on the final outcomes for the unit of study, Talia's students understood the reading and writing connection as well as the importance of keeping an organized and thorough data bank in service of the final writing task. To achieve these ends, it was important for Talia to formatively assess her students' progress throughout the unit by observing their levels of engagement and participation, recording notes while interacting with students during the lessons, and analyzing their written work. Mostly planning in advance yet leaving room for sudden aha's about student learning, Talia took daily informal notes in logs that she created with categories for the types of language and student behaviors she was seeing. She also planned each lesson to yield some form of written artifact that she could assess and use to provide feedback to students about their daily progress.

Formative assessment includes "all those activities undertaken by teachers—and by the students in assessing themselves—which provide information to

Talia created a folder for each student writing group with sections for reading, writing, speaking and listening, and language. Each section included the students' names with room for writing the date, the focus of the lesson, and notes. She focused on at least one group of students per lesson and wrote notes to track their progress. How do *you* record notes about student progress? Do you use running records, checklists, or another tool? You might talk to your colleagues about ways that you can capture what is happening as your students are learning in order to record progress toward specific learning outcomes.

be used as feedback to modify the teaching and learning activities in which they are engaged. Such assessment becomes formative when the evidence is actually used to adapt the teaching to meet students' needs" (Black & Wiliam, 1998, p. 140). A teacher's integrated use of formative assessment during instruction can provide immediate information to drive relevant and appropriate instruction. Talia's ongoing formative assessment practices illustrate an effort to hold herself accountable for assessing her students' learning and using her assessment processes to inform her instruction in a way that is responsive to the assets and needs of her culturally and linguistically diverse students.

Classroom Snapshot 2

Literary Analysis

Reading and understanding the themes in multicultural literature was part of Talia's backwards-planning process. One clear desired outcome for the written product was that students would be able to communicate their understanding of the theme(s) from a piece of literature in relation to the historical, social, political, or cultural context or the personal background of the author. In other words, students would both express their understanding of the themes from a literary text and explain how external contexts shaped and were reflected in the text.

During one of her reading lessons, for example, Talia led her class in a shared reading of Langston Hughes's "Thank you, M'am." She printed out copies of the short story with room for notes in the margins. The students took turns reading a paragraph or two at a time as Talia stopped them frequently to discuss the story, prompting the discussion with questions and pausing to allow students to record notes in the sidebars of the text. The questions Talia asked were specifically designed to help her multilingual students connect the events of the piece to historical contexts.

Talia began one discussion by pointing to a sentence in the text. "In this sentence, what do you think is happening in this quote: 'I were young once and I wanted things I could not get.' How is the story changing here?"

A few students suggested, "She remembers when she was young."

Talia asked, "Why do you think the author added this?"

Other students offered, "She starts to feel sorry for the boy."

Talia probed, "Do you think she's relating to the boy?"

"Yes," the students answered. One pointed out, using metalanguage the class had discussed earlier, "She uses dialectical language, too."

Talia continued, "Why do you think the author, Langston Hughes, chose to put the dialogue in dialectical language? What was the historical and cultural context of this short story? What were the *influences* of that time period on the author?

Remember the Harlem Renaissance?" Talia points to the reference chart they had created together around that time period in Harlem.

The students called out various responses:

"People were racist."

"Black people were down but coming up."

"I think the woman showed compassion for the boy because she knew he was hurt by racism and was poor just like her."

Talia wrapped up the discussion by commenting on their contributions. "What you all are doing right now is connecting what's happening in the text to the historical and social contexts. Let's write some of these notes together in our data banks." The students opened their writer's notebooks to the data bank for the story and started writing.

Although Talia conducted this exercise as a guided reading and note-taking task, as this dialogue makes clear, she also asked students to independently take notes as they read along. After walking around the room to check the students' notes, she determined that most were not writing comments as they read the piece. Consequently, when asked to list possible themes from the text, many either struggled to identify a theme or simply listed elements from the plot. Later, Talia shared that during her class discussion she realized this activity would need revision. Students were excited to contribute to the discussion but were confused about what to write for notes. As the period ended, she collected the students' papers to read them more carefully and expand her assessment of their progress.

Talia kept a running record in her class folders where she noted the frequency of students' contributions to the discussions, so she was able to compare this list with their written notes. A thoughtful read of each student's paper revealed to Talia that "my students made some connections but not enough. They also struggled to identify possible themes from the text." She recalled that many of the students who were enthusiastic during the class discussion had no notes on their papers except for those they had copied when she wrote with them. Talia determined that the class discussion had successfully fostered student engagement and some use of academic language, yet she realized that she hadn't provided explicit instruction on how students could transform their thinking into independently written notes.

Talia realized that she had not prepared her students adequately for the tasks she had given them. If she had simply moved on to the next lesson as prescribed by a curricular pacing guide, she would not have been able to do more explicit modeling to teach her students how to bridge from oral to written communication. Talia knew from her formative assessment during this lesson that her students were able to identify and respond to themes from literature. However, they needed support to take notes. Holding herself accountable for assessing her students' progress produced immediately applicable information.

Talia's next step was to plan an approach that would explicitly teach note-taking strategies and model ways to segue thinking about and discussing themes from literature into writing about themes from literature. As a result of this recognition, Talia prepared her document camera to project the text of the story so she could do a think-aloud to model discussion and note-taking strategies and how to use a graphic organizer. Talia explained, "I wanted to slowly walk students through the process of how to connect to the text. This way I could read the story aloud, do some think-aloud of my own, prompt a class discussion, then pause as students make specific connections of their own." Explicit instruction makes it easier to acquire the linguistic and cultural knowledge necessary to participate in the dominant culture for students like Talia's ELLs, who have not had much experience with the language and assumptions of school. Education scholar Lisa Delpit explains why: "Unless one has the leisure of a lifetime of 'immersion' to learn [the rules], explicit presentation makes learning immeasurably easier" (1988, p. 283).

Through ongoing formative assessment of her students, Talia evaluated her objectives and planned her daily teaching. Because she planned specific points in the reading to help students add to their data bank of notes, these also became the focal points for her formative assessment. For example, Talia would guide her students to specific places in the texts where the events or something the characters said or did reflected the themes of the story and prompt them with questions such as:

- What is happening here?
- Why do you think this is important in this piece?
- How does this relate to what has happened so far?
- What do you think is the significance of this?
- How does this event or quote connect to the historical, social, cultural, or political contexts of the time?

Each question promoted a discussion in pairs or small groups or as a whole class. Talia made notes on a chart as she floated around the room listening in on students' discussions. Later, Talia led a debrief, sharing what she had heard from listening to the discussions and modeling through a think-aloud to help students transfer their thinking and discussion into notes. The spot-checking informed her next lesson because she could see which students needed more support to write short notes in response to her questions. Figure 5.1 is an example of the note-taking and discussion grid that Talia's students used to organize their reading notes into a data bank that supported close analytical reading, discussion, and material for writing responses to literature.

Text Title: "Thank You, M'am" Excerpts/ quotes:	What is happening here?	Why do you think this is important in this piece?	How does this relate to what has happened so far?	What do you think is the significance of this?	How does this event or quote connect to the historical, social, cultural, or political contexts of the time?
"I were young once and I wanted things I could not get."	The lady is showing that she understands the boy's problems.	The lady and the boy were both poor.	The boy was scared of the lady but now she is nice.	Maybe the lady will not call the police.	The lady could relate to wanting things because she grew up in a racist society.
He did not trust the woman not to trust him. And he did not want to be mistrusted now.	Roger wants the lady to trust him.	Roger is changing.	At first Roger just wanted money, but now he wants the lady to trust him.	The lady was nice to Roger, so he wants to be nice back.	Kids are supposed to be respectful of old people, but Roger wasn't at first. Now he is being respectful.
"Now, here, take this ten dollars and buy yourself some blue suede shoes. And next time, do not make the mistake of latching onto my pocketbook nor nobody else's—because shoes come by devilish like that will burn your feet."	The lady gave Roger money to buy the shoes he wanted.	The lady is poor but gives Roger money.	Roger thought he had to steal money to get the shoes.	Roger learns about being nice to other people and not stealing.	Ten dollars was a lot of money for the lady and everyone then. But people also cared for their neighbors and helped them.

Figure 5.1. Sample data bank.

Classroom Snapshot 3

Experimenting with a Writing Formula: "The Full Meal Deal"

Through reading, discussion, and building a data bank, Talia's students had a thoughtful and thorough resource from which to draw evidence to support a response to literature thesis. It was time to begin the focus on writing the response to literature. Talia suspected from their past writing performance that her students would need support integrating evidence from their data banks into their responses to literature. For example, her school district had regular benchmark testing, so she had plenty of baseline data from her students' earlier responses to literature essays, showing, as she explained, "They tend to drop E-bombs—they just drop evidence—a quote from a source into their writing without really considering its appropriateness to the topic or without integrating the quote smoothly into the paragraph." She considered how she would teach a process for inserting and citing evidence from text, ultimately spending several days explicitly modeling and guiding students through a set of samples that featured what she called a "full meal deal," a formula for integrating examples from texts into pieces of writing. The "full meal deal" metaphor begins with an "appetizer," or thesis statement, topic sentence, opinion, or claim. The "entrée" is the evidence or example excerpted from the literature either as a direct or paraphrased quotation, properly cited. The "dessert" is the explanation or elaboration, usually in the form of commentary that explains the significance of the evidence or example.

Talia gave students the "full meal deal" in graphic form to help them understand the components of this formula for integrating text evidence into a written response to literature (see Figure 5.2). Talia's lesson included a detailed Power-Point slideshow that she presented as part of a whole-class modeling exercise (see examples in Figure 5.2). Throughout her process, Talia was apprehensive; she was concerned about this formulaic approach to writing and wasn't sure if even she herself believed it was a good idea to teach paragraph structure this way. Nonetheless, she knew her students well and knew they needed support to organize their thinking, their data, and their claims about the literature. However, she was still looking for a way to balance this standardized type of writing with the more flexible approach advocated in genre-based instruction.

The Full Meal Deal

Appetizer: Introduction of quote

Main Entrée: The quote or example paraphrased from the text

Dessert: Statement about the significance of the quote or example

Example *Full Meal Deal* paragraph written in response to the text "Thank You, M'am" by Langston Hughes:

Appetizer: Mrs. Jones allowed the boy into her house and from there, a train of events forever transformed the boy's behavior.

Main Entrée: She told him that, "Now, here take this ten dollars and buy yourself some blue suede shoes. And next time, do not make the mistake of latching onto *my* pocketbook, nor nobody else's—because shoes come by the devilish like that will burn your feet'" (Hughes, 33).

Dessert: When Mrs. Jones treated him with forgiveness and love, Roger realized his faulty choices of judgment. I believe he will never steal again.

Templates for Introducing Quotes	Templates for Analyzing Quotes
X states, "_____"	Basically, X is saying, _____
According to X, "_____"	In other words, X believes _____
X writes that "_____"	In making this comment, X argues that _____
In X's story/book, _____ X maintains that "_____"	The evidence shows that _____
	With this, X demonstrates that _____
In X's view, "_____"	
	X convinces me that _____
X agrees when s/he writes/says, "_____"	

Figure 5.2. The "full meal deal" formula.

Talia's uncertainty reflects the way many of us feel when we're trying something new with our students. The important thing is not that we feel one hundred percent certain about our teaching, but instead that we acknowledge the experimental nature of the teaching and learning processes. We can maintain our accountability to our students through formative assessment and adaptation along the way. Through formative assessment, Talia noticed that, while her students were now integrating evidence into their writing with commentary drawn from their data banks, their sentences all sounded the same, as if they were copied directly from the "full meal deal" samples.

To give her students a chance to operationalize the "full meal deal" and at the same time to investigate other ways to approach this work, Talia considered how to provide English language learners an opportunity to more fully understand the objectives of her explicit, somewhat formulaic writing instruction. She thought, "I need to give them a chance to be the evaluators, so they can grasp the purpose and the reason for integrating evidence—maybe by seeing [integrated evidence] through the eyes of the assessor they will come to understand the importance of supporting their claims with evidence from the text." Talia decided to engage her students in text analysis in the hopes that it would encourage students to develop deeper understandings about the purpose and the techniques of integrating evidence into their writing. According to assessment scholar D. Royce Sadler, to provide meaningful opportunities for students to become evaluators, "the learner has to (a) possess a concept of the standard being aimed for, (b) compare the current level of performance with the standard, and (c) engage in appropriate action which leads to some closure of the gap" (1989, p. 121). Talia had already delivered several days of direct instruction about the "full meal deal" and believed a text analysis activity would allow her to better assess what students could do independently.

Classroom Snapshot 4

Text Analysis: Moving Away from Formulaic Writing Instruction

Talia was interested in helping her English language learners understand some practical ways to structure their writing while providing them with options and decisions to make in a flexible GBI approach. Recognizing that real-world response to literature is different from the structure of school essays, she selected a variety of recommendations and reviews of books, movies, food, video games, and social media written by authors around the age of her students and published in magazines for kids. In keeping with the principles of genre-based instruction, Talia chose these texts carefully so they would present students with a variety of organizational structures and topics, but each also included some common features such as a recommendation or critique (the claim) and evidence to support the claim. Additionally, in all of the texts, the evidence was integrated smoothly and was appropriate and relevant to the claim. The organization, however, was different in each text. For example, in several the evidence came before the claim in a delayed thesis structure, while in other texts the structure was similar to the "full meal deal." This variety was intentional because Talia hoped her students would notice that although the order might be dissimilar, and there might be additional features, each of the elements of the "full meal deal" was present.

Talia supported her students in analyzing texts in a process authors John Bean, Virginia Chappell, and Alice Gillam call "descriptive outlining" in their book *Reading Rhetorically* (2014). Earlier in the year, Talia had introduced and unpacked some metalanguage, key verbs in a list adapted from *Reading Rhetorically*, posting these verbs on a large chart for students to reference. For example, some verbs describe what texts *do*: introduce, define, explain, oppose, support, question, and connect. Students can also be provided with graphic organizers or a simple T-chart (see Figure 5.3) for each text. Sentence stems can also support students in explaining what various sections of a text *say* and *do*.

To introduce her students to the ways in which responses to literature appear in the real world, Talia guided students through a learning activity to identify the parts of the texts she had selected. She then asked them to draw lines to separate the text into three or four parts (usually by paragraphs). Students worked in small collaborative groups to analyze each text. They responded to the following questions in the text analysis process:

- Why did you separate the text into the sections that you chose?
- In each section, what does the text *say*?
- In each section, what does the text *do?*
- Use some of the verbs from the verb chart to explain what each section of the text is *doing*.

Figure 5.3 is an example of a group's descriptive outline from reading a video game review.

After analyzing each text in their small groups, students presented their findings to the class. Each small group then evaluated their own decisions and the decisions made by their peers. As students engaged in these activities, Talia observed, walking around the classroom, answering questions, and stopping to help and prompt individual students. She used a running record sheet to check off which students were participating and took notes on some of what she heard them saying. Figure 5.4 is an example of a simple observation record sheet that Talia designed to record notes. She regularly adapted this record to focus on specific students or specific things she was looking for in her students' observations.

What does this section of the text *Say*?	What does this section of the text *Do*?
This is the most interesting video game on the market	*Introducing* the main focus of the text
Controlling movements in the game is so detailed	*Defining* terms like *analog control*
The games are unpredictable	*Reasoning* and evidence
Never boring and always full of surprises	*Explaining* why the reasons are important
Has all of the latest technology and is exciting no matter how much you play it	*Concluding* by summarizing the main ideas from the text

Figure 5.3. Sample video game review descriptive outline.

Student Name	Active Participation	Academic Language	Asking/Answering Questions

Figure 5.4. Observation recording sheet.

As she engaged her students in a whole-class debrief of the activity, Talia concluded that most of her students could identify the three main components of the "full meal deal," noting their location in the texts and, just as Talia had hoped, recognizing that they were not always in the same order in every text. Most important, Talia felt that all of her students were enthusiastic about their roles as evaluators and seemed to enjoy working in collaborative groups.

Talia's instruction was driven by daily formative assessment of her students *as they were actively engaged in learning*. She didn't wait until a later culminating assessment or use only test score data. In this way, she was able to experiment with formulaic writing instruction while maintaining the spirit of GBI and basing her pedagogical decisions on authentic and contextualized information. She had chosen to begin the writing instruction in this unit with the formulaic "full meal deal" because prior experience had revealed that this particular group of English language learners needed help recognizing and deploying the central moves of a response to literature text. This is a concern for many ELLs as well as other struggling writers who are not yet aware of how other writers use language to promote their perspectives. Had Talia started this unit with students evaluating real-world texts, they might not have been able to recognize the core moves when the texts were quite varied. However, Talia's decision to have students later evaluate real-world texts was essential to providing truly equitable instruction. Many classes that teach academic writing to ELLs stop when the students have mastered formulaic text structures (Enright & Gilliland, 2011). Students are left thinking that all texts written for that purpose must follow that exact pattern (Gilliland, 2012). While more fluent readers may be able to see how the moves vary in the texts they read, ELLs' smaller academic language and vocabulary knowledge can prevent them from grasping the distinctions. When Talia noticed her students' repeated use of the formulaic sentences and structures from the "full meal deal," she knew she had to shift her instruction.

Talia's assessment, based on her interactions with students' learning *as they were learning*, contributed to the design of immediate supports and extensions, which ultimately led to more engaging and collaborative activities for her students. Talia's developing knowledge of her students was based on learning which kinds of activities engaged and motivated them. She found that she could tap her students' prior experiences and knowledge by engaging them in class discussion and by regularly checking in with them as they were learning. Thus, her personal accountability process fostered better, more contextualized knowledge of her students. She documented that class discussion activities increased student participation, particularly among students who had not been previously participating. These class discussions afforded her English language learners the opportunity to develop their ideas verbally so that they would be better prepared to express these ideas in writing.

Classroom Snapshot 5

Peer Feedback and Revision

After the text analysis lessons, Talia presented her students with options. She invited them to choose one story from those they had read in the Voices in Multicultural Literature unit. Referencing past lessons on discourse-level concerns in texts, she next asked the students to choose their purpose, audience, and context so they could respond to the writing task. Once they had selected these foci, students then chose the structure of their texts. For example, in the preceding text analysis lessons, they had analyzed several published recommendations and reviews in literary and news-oriented magazines for youth. They noticed that some texts, like the recommendations, were persuasive and encouraged readers to buy the product, read the book, or see the movie. Other texts were more informative and explanatory in nature and did not stem from an opinion, but instead introduced and provided information about a book, movie, or product. Talia invited her students to choose the purpose for writing about the themes in their selected text: would they recommend or critique the text through persuasion, or would they inform their audience about the themes in the text? Next, in terms of audience, would they be writing to their peers? Parents and teachers? Broader audiences? Based on their audiences, what types of language would be appropriate? Finally, students chose the appropriate format for their context. Would their writing be published in a magazine like the ones they had analyzed earlier, or would they put their writing in the form of a school-based assignment, like an essay? How would they then structure their text to fit their context?

There were no right or wrong approaches, and Talia supported students in making these choices through graphic organizers and other visual outlining resources, which helped to highlight the differences between the options. The assessment criteria remained the same: the final written product needed to contain a claim or thesis about the theme(s) from the text, evidence, and analysis or explanation. These three criteria were located in every text students had previously analyzed in their text analysis lessons. They could choose to add other elements they had seen in the recommendations they analyzed, such as a counterargument or a call to action, but these additions would not be assessed this time. Once they had written the first drafts, Talia supported their revision process. One of her interests was in building students' ability to notice how texts could be improved. Talia wanted her ELLs to develop editing and revision skills both for their own writing and for test-taking purposes.

> Many assessments, including some of the items in the Smarter Balanced Assessment Consortium item bank, include pieces of writing for students to edit. Items ask, for example, "What word fits better in sentence 1?" We see these editing skills as also important for students' own revision processes: by engaging in these types of editing processes for their own and their peers' writing, students presumably will be better prepared when they encounter these types of tasks on assessments. We address preparation for standardized tests in more detail in Chapter 6.

One way for teachers to introduce students to processes and skills for providing feedback for revision purposes is to co-construct comprehensible criteria for looking at a piece of writing. Talia wrote two responses to a literary text that had not been included in the students' options, one an exemplar of what could be expected from the prompt and the other not fully addressing the assessment requirements. After reading the exemplar she had created, Talia engaged her students in several layers of analysis. For example, they interactively discussed the following concepts:

- The impact of the whole piece on the reader
- The ways in which certain selected paragraphs supported the overall meaning
- How particular sentences were structured to convey meaning
- The impact of single word choices

Talia led her students through the same process with the less successful text she had created, asking them to think about and discuss the differences between the two responses to literature. She prompted them to identify traits in the writing that worked in the exemplar and were missing in the other sample and supported them as they came up with metalanguage such as *imagery*, *descriptive language*, and *sensory details*. Talia created a reference chart (see the sidebar below) for students to use when providing feedback to their peers.

Talia's text analysis lessons provided scaffolding and language support so that her English language learners could access higher-order thinking and learning opportunities. This is critical for equity teaching because *all* students should have opportunities for critical thinking and rigorous learning experiences as well as the language support to get there. Furthermore, by focusing on revision, Talia sought

During the early months of the school year, much of the language that Talia's students used in text analysis activities was informal, but over time it developed into academic language when students had fully operationalized the more accessible language. For example, the class brainstormed a list of effective characteristics from one of the first texts they read together. Talia recorded the following:

1. Clear, and makes sense

2. Funny

3. Makes me think of pizza

Talia then led her students through the process of transforming the initial reference chart into a second list that translated the initial brainstormed list into academic language:

1. The writing flows from topic to topic in a logical, organized format or structure.

2. The word choices are appropriate to the purpose and intended audience of the piece.

3. The imagery is compelling and/or thought-provoking.

In this way, Talia supported students' bridging from the "known" to the "new" by accessing their prior knowledge about characteristics of effective texts. Starting from informal metalanguage and creating a bridge to academic metalanguage is a key consideration when working with English language learners. The reference chart they created together served as a starting point for looking at one another's writing and providing peer feedback.

to support and build her students' perceptions of themselves as writers and as peers capable of providing meaningful feedback to one another.

Talia used the teacher-created samples and the list of criteria for effective writing that the class had generated to move her students to the next step in providing peer feedback. They began by critiquing the teacher-created samples in order to practice using some of the language needed for feedback and revision. This way, the students learned to analyze writing without the added pressure of sharing their own writing or critiquing one another's writing. Talia introduced her students to the same TAG structure Gary had used for peer feedback (*Tell* something you like, *Ask* questions, and *Give* a suggestion). The TAG structure was designed to hold students accountable for participating and to give the teacher a written product to assess the nature of the peer feedback, along with her observation notes. Having implemented the TAG conferences a few times, Talia noticed that her students were pretty successful at giving feedback. After collecting written products of their work throughout the peer feedback process, however, she noticed that much of what the peers suggested, even what she considered appropriate feedback, was not making it into students' revised drafts. The suggestions were sound, but the revised pieces were quite similar to the first drafts, aside from some spelling and punctuation changes. Talia determined through her formative assessment that she needed to design a way to support students in incorporating the feedback their peers provided.

Talia explained how she gained insight into her next instructional steps based on what she saw in her students' class participation and writing. Sharing a piece of writing from one of her students, she pointed out, "They mostly revised for grammar, spelling, organization, and word choice." Once she discovered that these were her students' main foci, Talia wanted to give them opportunities to reflect on this feedback and evaluate these revisions so they could identify other ways to respond to their peers' writing and revise their own work.

As a result of gathering this information about her students' writing, Talia designed a lesson to co-construct with the whole class a list titled "Ideas for Revision Suggestions" that students would put in the tool kit section in their writer's notebooks. Together as a class, the students brainstormed additions to their initial list of traits of effective writing. Talia discussed with them "different kinds of changes that are possible so you have an idea of a variety of things to look for in each other's writing besides punctuation, spelling, and other conventions." Figure 5.5 is the revision checklist that Talia co-created with her students.

In addition to co-constructing the checklist to use during peer conferencing, Talia built feedback into the accountability process. For example, she asked students to consider the feedback they had been given, select which feedback to incorporate into their revisions, and explain their revision decisions. Talia told her

Questions	Feedback for Improvement
Does the writing make sense?	
Does the author's voice match the task?	
Does the language (word choices) fit the task?	
Does the writing have an organized, logical flow?	
Is the text the right length?	
Is there imagery that is thought-provoking or compelling?	
Does the writing stay on topic/focused?	
Any issues with grammar, punctuation, spelling, or formatting?	

Figure 5.5. Revision checklist compiled by Talia and her students.

students, "If you make changes based on what your peers and what you yourself have determined are important and necessary, this makes you the experts, instead of me saying, 'You must change this because this is a better way according to me the teacher.'" Furthermore, Talia asked her students, "Who is the ultimate author of this essay? You. When people give you feedback, why are they giving you this feedback? To help you improve something . . . but who is the ultimate author? You. Sometimes people are going to give you feedback, and you may not agree with it, and that's okay. You don't have to make every change that's suggested. But if you've been given feedback from a variety of readers and yet you don't make any changes, I am going to ask you to tell me why."

Reflection: Using Information from Student Work to Inform Practice

The multilayered data sets that Talia collected and analyzed after several rounds of peer feedback and reflecting on revisions provided a more complete picture of her students' growth from the beginning of the process than she could have seen from just looking at their final drafts. Her assessment data included her students' first drafts of their responses to literature and their self-reflections prior to sharing their writing with their peers. She also collected the peer feedback that students had received for the writing they shared in their TAG conferences, with each of the peers' suggestions highlighted in pink. Talia further collected the revised drafts of each of her students' writing in which they had highlighted their revisions in green, reflected on each of the revisions they had made, and explained why they made each revision.

Additionally, Talia compared on-demand benchmark writing assessments from earlier in the year to student writing that was part of an ongoing process of active reading, discussion, text analysis, language supports, and revision. The differences between the two were, unsurprisingly, immense. For example, the on-demand writing that Talia analyzed contained very little if any evidence drawn from the text to support the claims. Instead, students had either written very little or brought in ideas from their own thinking that were not drawn from the text they had been asked to read. In their process writing, by contrast, students more elaborately supported their claims with relevant evidence drawn from the texts they had read. Talia could also see the impact of feedback on their revisions, as almost every student changed at least one thing about their writing in response to peer and teacher feedback.

The analysis of student writing provided Talia with the opportunity to understand how her students engaged in process writing, as well as how they had grown in their thinking and writing. She explained how she graded these multilay-ered written products: "The grade weighs heavier due to the *growth*. I based the grades on students' reflections so that they would understand that it was the *reflec-tion* and the *thinking* that was key, not the writing itself necessarily." Talia reflected on how flexible grouping worked for her students. "All of these kids are in the same writing group, and this girl," she pointed to an essay sample, "is an example of putting a higher-achieving student in a struggling group. It actually worked well for everyone. She helped them, and they helped her, too. This brought everyone in that group up."

Through focused formative assessment at intentional and targeted points in her teaching, Talia developed an increasingly challenging, metacognitive repertoire of teaching strategies. She engaged her students as evaluators of various types of texts, including their own writing, their peers' writing, the peer feedback they had been given, and the revisions that responded to the feedback. Thus, her pedagogy incorporated several layers of critical thinking and metacognition that would not have been responsive to her specific students' assets and learning needs if she had not engaged in focused and intentional formative assessment along the way. Talia had plenty of concrete samples of student work that showed learning and growth. She collected these artifacts in portfolios to share with students' parents and the school staff to show how her English language learners were progressing in their reading, writing, and language development.

Through each of her text analysis and peer feedback rounds, Talia strength-ened her own and her students' understanding that reading, writing, speaking, listening, and language development are linked. Just as Bean and colleagues (2014) note, writing as you read is an essential aspect of active reading. Integrated with discussion and focused attention to the language of a given text, writing while reading can support ELL students in building their reading skills as well as generating a wealth of ideas (captured in a data bank) for writing tasks, which are designed in response to the actively read texts. Skilled rhetorical readers might write in the margins of a text and record notes in a reading log, journal, or computer document. Sometimes rhetorical readers stop reading in the middle of a passage and freewrite their ideas in progress. Writing while reading both supports comprehension and inspires students toward invention as they generate ideas while interacting with a text. Teachers who are prepared, as Talia was, to stop, prompt, assess, and make necessary shifts throughout the reading of texts may experience the same success she had in her classroom. As we've noted elsewhere in this book, these are practices that benefit all students. English language learners, however, often rely more on school as the main source of their English language input. From an equity perspective, explicitly teaching ELLs how to read for writing while also guiding their language development gives them an equal opportunity to learn from reading and demonstrate their understanding through writing. The appendix on page 149 provides suggestions for additional ways to integrate language-focused lessons into your teaching.

Texts do many things and work in many ways. The examples in this book show how teachers can engage their students in analyzing texts for their organizational structures, purposes, intended audiences, language, content, and contexts. The students in Talia's class analyzed literary texts for theme and how themes connect to the historical and cultural contexts in which the texts were conceived and produced. Talia's class also analyzed informational and opinion texts (recommendations and critiques) in order to see how writers smoothly integrate evidence from another source into their own writing. In Chapter 6, we describe how Rachel, Gary, and Talia's language-focused GBI approach to text analysis, which supported their English language learners in gaining metalinguistic awareness, also serves as preparation for standardized tests.

Demonstrating Accountability and Equity beyond the Classroom

Assessment: How Genre-Based Instruction Prepares Multilingual Students for High-Stakes Tests

If students bring their knowledge of the purpose, structure, and grammatical characteristics of genres to the assessment situation then they will have an advantage as this can ensure less of a gap between assessment material and students' real life target situations.

—Paltridge, 2001, p. 87

At Willowdale High School (WHS) in California's Central Valley, district curriculum planners recognized that their students were not doing well on the essay portion of the California High School Exit Examination (CAHSEE). Each essay task was selected from one of four possible text types: biographical narrative, persuasive essay, response to literature, and expository composition. While the WHS English curriculum had faithfully followed a textbook program that aligned carefully with the state standards and therefore the diverse tasks tested on the annual standardized test, students struggled with the on-demand writing portion of the exit exam.[10] To better prepare them for this part of the test, the district implemented a set of benchmark assignments for ninth- and tenth-grade English language arts classes. Each benchmark assignment was what the district called a "process essay," written in response to a task similar to those on the CAHSEE. Evelyn Chou and her colleagues teaching English 9, English 10, and advanced

English language development classes were required to have their students complete the benchmark assignment essays by set dates across the school year, at which point the teachers graded the essays on a district-established rubric. In general, they devoted between two and four weeks to each benchmark assignment essay, scaffolding students' prewriting, planning, and drafting process. By the end of the unit, the students had a polished multiparagraph essay that met the requirements on the rubric (Gilliland, 2017).

In theory, these assignments should have been ideal preparation for the timed exam since they followed the same formats and were judged on similar rubrics. In practice, however, they did little to support students' ability to succeed on the essay exam, for two primary reasons: (1) the scaffolding, while it enabled students to write passing essays, did not include teaching students *about* the writing process or the genre, and (2) the circumstances under which the essays were written were completely different from those of the exam (with the benchmark assignments, there were no time limits, the teachers provided substantial scaffolding of the writing process, and students revised several times based on teacher feedback). So far in this book, we have discussed ways that language-focused GBI can address the first concern by helping students understand the writing process and how to write independently. This chapter takes on the second challenge of preparing students for the circumstances of high-stakes assessments, including on-demand timed writing.

As the teachers featured in Chapters 3, 4, and 5 demonstrate, a careful emphasis at Willowdale High School on GBI and the language of genres could have considerably limited the problems that follow from not providing students with an awareness of the process or genre while still helping students do better on standardized measures. For example, Rachel Easton understood that it was critical to prepare her students for the high-stakes assessments they would have to take. Such assessments were part of the criteria for students' retention and their placement in both middle and high school English classes. Test scores also determined whether students would be redesignated or placed in extra "support" classes, often at the expense of an elective. Rachel provided test preparation by engaging her students in critical thinking about texts throughout the school year instead of as an add-on right before students took the test. She was primarily motivated to provide fun and engaging critical thinking and writing experiences for her students so they could build a variety of skills useful for both school and life. However, she also believed that engaging students in thorough and sustained investigations of texts would prepare students to analyze the texts and tasks they would encounter in an assessment situation.

In this chapter, we return to accountability concerns with the performance of English language learners on high-stakes standardized tests. While throughout the book we have highlighted how teacher practices can support and evaluate

ELLs' learning of the skills and practices emphasized in the Common Core State Standards and other state standards related to academic literacy, at this point we turn specifically to standardized testing. We consider how teachers can help their multilingual students be better prepared for the literacy demands of quarterly and annual standardized assessments, high school exit exams, and college entrance and placement tests (such as the SAT). Although we strongly discourage courses focused entirely on preparing students for standardized tests (courses into which many multilingual high school students are placed), we advocate here for *reasonable* "teaching the test" as an equity issue, since research has shown that ELLs are often unfamiliar with testing formats and procedures (Sandberg & Reschly, 2011). The primary gist of the chapter, however, is to show how teachers have applied the principles of genre theory and functional language illustrated in previous chapters in ways that make connections between real-world literacy and formal tests of reading and writing.

With respect to issues of accountability, GBI addresses lesson planning, teaching, and assessment in ways that give teachers opportunities to maximize real-world learning at the same time as they prepare students for high-stakes assessments. A genre-centered approach, according to genre scholar Ann Johns, is "an approach in which literacy classes become laboratories for the study of texts, roles, and contexts . . . where students develop strategies for future rhetorical situations" (1997, p. 19). These future rhetorical situations, for ELLs in US schools, will almost certainly include taking standardized tests and on-demand writing assessments. When students understand that standardized tests are themselves academic genres and that these genres are different in important ways from other texts they have read and written in class, they can better apply their ability to analyze genres to maximize their performance on the tests.

Standardized Testing

Standardized testing has become a way of life in US schools, but mainstream teachers may not be aware that students designated as English language learners are subjected to more assessments than are their English-fluent peers. Adolescent ELLs must take not only the same standardized tests as their classmates, but also additional tests that determine their status as English language learners. In this section, we briefly review the many tests that multilingual students may encounter as they progress through secondary school and on to college.

When parents enroll a child in a new school, they are asked to fill out a home language survey that asks what languages their child speaks with various family members. Federal law gives schools thirty days to assess new arrivals whose parents indicated on their intake form that they speak a language other than English at home. English language proficiency (ELP) exams differ from state to state, but they are required to be administered annually to all students who are currently classified as English language learners, as well as to newcomers. The format of these tests varies but usually includes oral and written English for both daily and academic purposes. One of the most commonly used ELP tests is the ACCESS test developed by WIDA, which assesses reading, writing, listening, and speaking within the context of school content areas. Other states have developed their own ELP tests that cover similar language content.

As they move through their schooling, multilingual students also take the annual standardized assessments that are required under federal law in English language arts, math, and science. These tests are mostly multiple-choice (selected response) format and may also include short written responses (constructed response) and longer written responses or on-demand timed essays (performance tasks). In some districts, students also take quarterly benchmark assessments. More than half of US states have instituted policies that in addition to meeting all course credit requirements, students must pass a high school exit exam that includes English and mathematics.[11] As we explore in the next section, the structure and linguistic complexity of both annual tests and exit exams can be a challenge for multilingual students who know the content but are still developing their academic English proficiency.

Those students who intend to continue their education after high school will also face a battery of additional standardized tests for college admissions and placement. Most four-year colleges require some form of standardized test scores to be submitted with the application; the SAT and ACT are most common. Students who graduate from a US high school but have studied here for less than two or three years may be required to take the TOEFL (Test of English as a Foreign Language) as part of their admissions requirements. Once admitted, students are required by many two- and four-year colleges to take an English placement test before beginning their first term. The placement test score can determine whether they have to take developmental English language or writing courses before first-year composition or whether they are placed in ESL or "native speaker" sections. Some colleges also set a time limit for how long students can remain enrolled before meeting a standard (such as one year to place into first-year composition).

Clearly, standardized tests hold high stakes for multilingual students throughout their secondary school education and beyond. It is therefore essential for teachers to help their students learn how to show what they know when they come face to face with such potentially difficult but highly influential tests.

Why Are Standardized Tests a Challenge for ELLs?

Standardized tests hold high stakes for all students, but those classified as English language learners face greater challenges in proving their knowledge and abilities on such exams. Their performance on these tests can determine whether they are placed into college prep or remedial courses (Patthey, Thomas-Spiegel, & Dillon, 2009), whether they receive needed special education services or are wrongly diagnosed as needing these services (Abedi, 2006; Sullivan, 2011), and whether they are supported to stay in school or drop out (Sandberg & Reschly, 2011). Until recently, few standardized tests were normed with English language learners, which means that while the test scores may validly represent what fluent English speakers know, they cannot be accepted as evidence of ELLs' abilities. Discrepancies in multilingual students' test scores can be attributed to many factors.

While many multilingual students may not have had the opportunity to learn the content being tested due to recent arrival in the United States or frequent family moves across school districts (Olsen, 2010), others who know the content may still not be able to show what they know in English (Jones & Egley, 2007). The format of the test itself can be an obstacle since multiple-choice items and bubble sheets are not used everywhere in the world. In addition, new Internet-based tests require computer skills, which puts at a disadvantage students who don't have computers at home or don't have experience with item formats such as drag-and-drop or check-all-that-apply. Furthermore, many students don't have the keyboarding skills required to type short or lengthy responses to assessment tasks administered on the computer.

Of even greater concern for multilingual learners is the language of the test itself. Considerable research analyzing the language of standardized tests has shown that test questions are often confusing to multilingual students not because of the content but because of the way the questions are written. When students don't understand what the question is asking, they can't demonstrate that they know the answer to the question. This then makes the questions invalid for showing students' content knowledge in all academic subjects. Some of the linguistic structures that have been found to be particularly difficult for English learners are the following:

> • *Unfamiliar words and idioms.* Because they are still learning English in general, multilingual students are at a disadvantage when test questions use low-frequency or specialized words and idioms. Longer words are often less common and therefore more challenging for learners. Even terms that are culturally relevant to one population could be unclear to students from other cultural groups (such as an Arabic-speak-

ing student trying to answer a question that mentions tacos and enchiladas). For example, if a sentence begins "The words on the marquee read . . . ," students who are unfamiliar with the word *marquee* might not be able to picture what is being described.

• *Complex sentences, especially those using relative and subordinating clauses, conditionals, and logical connectors.* In addition to simply being longer, these structures are less commonly used in spoken English and are often structured differently in English than they are in other languages, so students may have more trouble understanding what is meant. For example, contrast these two uses of the word *while*: (1) "While they were baking cookies, the phone rang." (2) "While Sally wants to help her friend, she does not know how." In the first sentence, *while* is used to indicate that one activity (baking cookies) was going on during the time that another occurred (the telephone rang). In the second sentence, it indicates a contrast between Sally's desire to help and her ability to do so. Both create logical relationships between clauses, and the reader needs to understand how the activities are related; the two different meanings of *while* add to a novice reader's confusion.

• *Long verb or noun phrases, including prepositional phrases.* These structures can interfere with a reader's ability to identify who is doing what, especially when they are used in a question. For example, a question asking students to interpret the meaning of a text might ask: "Which of the following is the best approximation of the detective's reasons for taking a photograph of the scientific measuring equipment?" Here we have four prepositional phrases and a long noun phrase (scientific measuring equipment), each of which adds a level of confusion for readers who may not even understand what their task is. Another potential problem for ELLs with multiple-choice questions that ask, "Which of the following is the best . . ." is that more than one option may be possible if they didn't fully understand the reading passage, as these questions are often written with the wrong choices drawn from the text as well.

• *Voice of verb phrases.* Passive voice questions are more difficult to understand, especially when they obscure the actor. Compare the clarity of "The books were placed on the shelf" with "Sandra put the books on the shelf." Learners may struggle to picture what is going on in the first sentence.

• *Negation.* In English a double negative means a positive, but in other languages, adding more negative words can amplify the negation. Thus, a Spanish speaker might misinterpret "Nobody at the party did not have some fun" as meaning "Nobody at the party had fun."

• *Exclusion questions asking the test taker to identify what is NOT part of a group.* While students might be able to identify the correct answers, if they don't understand that they are being asked to select the one response that is wrong, they may be confused about how to respond. For example, upon seeing a question asking, "Which of the following is not an example the author gave?," students who had struggled to understand the reading passage might be relieved to see at least one item they recognize as coming from the passage and will mark that as their response. (Abedi, 2006; Abedi & Gándara, 2006; Kopriva, 2000; Solano-Flores & Trumbull, 2003)

In addition to the language demands at the sentence level, standardized tests require students to access literacy skills in multiple domains. Reading passages can range in length from one paragraph to multiple pages and may also include additional features such as graphs, maps, or charts. Tasks in response to reading include comprehension questions asking students to identify information provided in the passage and inference questions that require drawing conclusions about information beyond the provided passage, such as identifying the author's purpose or guessing what information would be included in the next chapter of a story. Students might also be asked to use multiple literacy skills to compare two different texts, including reading a text and a graph, or a chart and a map. Many of these question formats can be extra difficult for English language learners whose language proficiency is not strong enough to fully comprehend the reading passage, let alone represent an awareness of the author's reasons for writing.

Writing for standardized assessments usually takes the form of timed essays written to a specific prompt or task. Some test questions ask students to draw on their own experiences to support an argument or illustrate a claim, while others provide materials that students should include as they write their response. For example, the California High School Exit Exam included one written essay task, which could either be a text analysis response to a reading passage or a response to a question in which students took a stand on an issue. Similarly, the TOEFL has two writing tasks: one asks students to take a stand on a universal issue such as whether college students should live at home or in a dormitory; the other requires a synthesis of a listening passage (usually in the form of a brief college-style lecture) and a reading passage on the same topic but with a different perspective. Although these writing tasks are intended to be accessible to students no matter their background, they put additional burdens on multilingual learners whose earlier education may not have covered the concepts that are assumed to be common knowledge, or who do not have the cultural background to comprehend the reading passage.

The examples in Figure 6.1 demonstrate how different state writing exams can be challenging for multilingual learners. The Arizona seventh-grade AIMS task assumes that students will have had experience going to movie theaters, will understand what a "discount movie theater" is, and care that one is closing. On the CAHSEE task, the story students must analyze is a two-page narrative of a teenage boy hiking in the desert with his father and brother. Students whose lived experiences have not included leisurely family camping trips or who cannot visualize the desert environment could struggle to make general sense of the passage and not be able to focus on the literary elements in the text. The New York Regents Exam requires students to compare two texts that include references to American cultural icons from many years ago and then analyze them for theme and literary elements.

The constraints of timed writing tasks create a genre of text that contrasts greatly with the real-world genres students may have studied in English classes. Additionally, the rubrics used for assessing these texts are developed to ensure reliable scoring procedures and often focus more on structure and grammatical accuracy than on creativity. Because this scoring is usually done anonymously in a mass reading by trained human scorers or by computer programs designed to recognize specific features and grammatical errors (or sometimes by both humans and computers), essays that stick as closely as possible to the rubric score highest. The rubrics often fit well with the five-paragraph essay structure. Writing scholar George Hillocks (2002) notes that these constraints mean that timed writing assessment rewards shallow, formulaic texts rather than those that show individuality or take risks.

Figure 6.1. Sample writing tasks from released items on state standardized tests.[12]

Arizona AIMS seventh grade: Going to the movies is a major source of entertainment for many students. Imagine that the only discount movie theater in your area is closing. Write a persuasive essay in support of keeping the discount movie theater open.

California CAHSEE response to reading: In the story "The Hiking Trip," the reader learns about the main character, Jeff. Jeff's personality and emotions are revealed through the actions and dialogue presented in the story. Write an essay in which you describe the personality and emotions of Jeff, the main character. How do his personal characteristics add to the events in the story? How does the author reveal this information about Jeff in the story? Use details and examples from the story to support your ideas.

New York Regents Exam: Read the passages on the following pages (a poem and an excerpt from an essay) about possessions. . . . (1) Write a well-developed paragraph in which you use ideas from both passages to establish a controlling idea about possessions. Develop your controlling idea using specific examples and details from each passage. (2) Choose a specific literary element (e.g., theme, characterization, structure, point of view, etc.) or literary technique (e.g., symbolism, irony, figurative language, etc.) used by one of the authors. Using specific details from that passage, in a well-developed paragraph, show how the author uses that element or technique to develop the passage

---

In addition to learning how to write to the specifications of an exam essay, multilingual students need to learn time management strategies for taking such tests. Unlike in the classroom, they can't spend much time brainstorming ideas or discussing their thoughts with peers or their teachers; instead they have to focus on how to include the first appropriate ideas they think of into a set format and how to structure their paragraphs to fit the requirements of the rubric. While writing, they also need to monitor the time to make sure to wrap up and take a few minutes to proofread.

Test-taking procedures often contrast with the learning methods of regular classroom time and can put greater stress on multilingual students. High-stakes assessments almost always require individual work and prohibit collaboration or asking for help from the teacher. Although federal and state policy suggests that schools should provide accommodations for students classified as English language learners, these accommodations are often in the form of a glossary or use of a dictionary, which means students need to know how to look up words quickly. Many tests also forbid writing in the test booklet; although this constraint can be challenging for all students, multilingual learners can struggle even more. Making sense of complex test questions can take up a lot of mental energy, leaving fewer resources for eliminating choices. Additionally, many of the new year-end tests are conducted on computers, adding the challenge of having adequate keyboarding skills to type essays and mouse skills to complete drag-and-drop tasks. Students, including those from many low-income immigrant families, who haven't had experience using desktop computers may struggle with basic computer skills.

All of the issues we have outlined in this section contribute to the limited validity of standardized tests with respect to fair and valid assessment of English language learners. We see these limitations as an equity concern, not least because they bear extremely high stakes for multilingual students who may end up being wrongly placed in a course or denied a high school diploma because they didn't understand the language of the test. While there are approved accommodations for multilingual students taking standardized tests, these accommodations are frequently inadequate for students to show what they really know. It is our responsibility as teachers to advocate for our ELL students at school and in the community, stressing how much they *do* know that is not captured in these tests.

Accommodations for Multilingual Learners

Accommodations for ELLs are often recommended or required by state testing policy. These accommodations may include material support such as a bilingual glossary or environmental accommodations such as letting ELLs have extra time or take the test in a separate room. When giving students summative assessments during the school year, we can provide some additional accommodations that will make the process more equitable and allow them to demonstrate their knowledge of the content being assessed. Some accommodations might include clarifying for students how they can make use of the extra time they have and what the requirements are for specific test items (Kopriva, 2000). Teachers might be allowed to explain the context of passages that are culturally American (such as a question about baseball or Thanksgiving). It may help students with stronger oral than literacy abilities to hear an aide read the directions or test items aloud; other students might benefit from receiving a test with the items written in "plain English," with simpler sentence structure and vocabulary (Abedi, 2010; Kopriva, 2000). Kopriva also suggests that students might be allowed to answer open-ended test questions with drawings or charts instead of being restricted to writing in complete sentences.

> Accommodations are important to ELLs because they represent their best chance for performing well on tests administered in a language they do not fully understand. If high stakes tests are not going to go away, and test developers and education policy makers are going to insist on using tests with this student population, then two issues need to be addressed for ELLs. First, their inclusion in high stakes tests needs to be considered relative to accommodations, . . . making sure issues of validity and fairness are addressed. Second, educational placement, promotion, and graduation policies based on results and inferences from the high stakes tests need to be reconsidered. In fact, the only ethical purpose for using an English language test with ELLs would be to inform instruction, not to determine academic achievement levels, and surely not to punish and humiliate students, parents, teachers, and administrators. (Solórzano, 2008, p. 310)

Assessment specialist Ronald Solórzano (2008) notes, however, that problems persist if students don't know how to use the accommodations (such as a bilingual dictionary or computer), or if the accommodation doesn't maintain the same intent as the original (such as a poor translation into the student's home language). For example, if students don't have grade-level literacy in their first language, they may not be able to make use of a bilingual dictionary to understand the intent of the test question. Allowing students to write essay responses in their home languages would be an appropriate response *if* students are able to write at grade level in those languages *and* there is a scorer available who is bilingual in those languages and English (Kopriva, 2000). Scoring ELLs' responses can also be a problem if the readers are not prepared to separate linguistic errors from students' demonstration of content knowledge. These concerns mean that we need to be careful with accommodations so they still allow students to demonstrate their knowledge of the content we are trying to assess.

The Genres of Testing

Although as teachers most of us have little control over the content or presentation of the high-stakes tests our multilingual students must take, we do have the power to prepare them for the tests in ways that help them learn. One aspect of accountability is helping students understand how the tests are structured so they can demonstrate to the best of their ability what they *do* know in English—in other words, making sure that the test measures their content knowledge rather than their test-taking abilities. To this extent, we advocate understanding assessments as a genre and as such, argue for integrating some test-taking practice into other literacy learning throughout the school year so the tests aren't a strange format that surprises learners when they open the test booklet. This does not mean that we suggest teaching entirely to the test but rather that we acknowledge that standardized test format is in itself a genre, and therefore teaching students about this genre should be one of many different ways that teachers are accountable to their students and to the community.

Helping Students Understand Standardized Tests

Teaching to the test doesn't have to mean (as it too often has been interpreted) narrowing the curriculum to a focus on the surface-level features that high-stakes tests assess. Education researchers Vicky Giouroukakis and Andrea Honigsfeld (2010) observed English language arts and English language development teachers at four high schools in Long Island, New York, to see how they approached preparing their multilingual students for the state's high stakes Regents Exam, which serves as both an achievement test and a high school exit exam. The teachers admitted to feeling pressure to prepare their students for the test, but they implemented their "teaching to the test" through meaningful practices that both helped students develop metalinguistic and metacognitive test-taking abilities and supported them in building their literacy knowledge for purposes beyond the test. We return to the classroom of Talia Fenton to illustrate some of the findings from Giouroukakis and Honigsfeld's research study, approaches we have also observed her and other teachers implementing in classrooms across the country. We consider how her practices introduced students to the language and genres of the tests without hurting their opportunities to learn how to use reading, writing, and language for real-world purposes.

One way Talia supported her multilingual students was by bringing aspects of the test into her day-to-day teaching. For example, she used culturally and linguistically responsive practices in lessons to help students develop literacy skills appropriate to taking tests: teaching both everyday and content-specific vocabulary; supporting writing with sentence, paragraph, and essay frames and graphic organizers; and encouraging students to use peer interaction, their home languages, and their funds of knowledge to increase their comprehension of texts. While these supports wouldn't be permitted on the actual day of the test, by using them throughout the academic year, Talia's students had a lot of practice unpacking writing prompts, tasks, and rubric criteria in order to respond appropriately to test items. The genre study they pursued throughout the school year helped the students develop real-world literacy skills that could also help on the test: note taking, reading for different purposes, and interpreting charts were among the skill-development practices Talia and her lesson study colleagues Rachel Easton and Gary Miller used. Purposeful selection of culturally relevant texts and authentic materials that students could relate to allowed them to practice new literacy skills with familiar content. To help students make meaning from less familiar texts, Talia incorporated a variety of additional approaches:

- Facilitating students' use of oral language to understand and show their comprehension of written texts, such as by acting out scenes from stories.
- Responding to movie adaptations of literary works and radio interviews with authors and actors to draw on students' oral language strengths.
- Using creative writing and drawing to connect to the themes of literary or informational texts.
- Focusing vocabulary lessons on words and phrases that appear regularly in the test questions and instructions.
- Practicing task analysis and outlining with released test questions and test-taking strategy practice, such as eliminating less likely distractors on a multiple-choice item.

Talia regularly took the time to teach students specifically about the tests they would be taking and how they could understand tasks and show their knowledge. Especially for intermediate and lower-proficiency ELLs, Talia created her own mock testing materials to scaffold students' learning about the genre of the test and to prepare them for taking the actual test. Some of these mock tests simplified directions and language to scaffold students' practice with test tasks; others provided sentence starters or graphic organizers to enable students to produce an appropriate written response. At times throughout the year, students responded to writing tasks with an outline or a single paragraph instead of a complete essay in order to practice the process of planning. Lower-proficiency students could practice their responses orally, or use a dictionary or their home language in constructing their response. Talia's teacher-created mock tests presented culturally responsive materials (such as texts on topics of relevance to students' lives) with the same task types as those found on the tests. Having extra time during practice tests also allowed students to show what they knew about content. Giouroukakis and Honigsfeld note that these approaches help students by "enhancing their metacognitive and metalinguistic awareness as well as test-taking skills" (2010, p. 484). These approaches contribute to equitable learning experiences for multilingual students by reducing their anxiety about taking the test while also supporting them in approaching the tasks more confidently.

Talia implemented three simultaneous teaching practices that contribute to a positive form of teaching to the test, summed up as:

- Purposeful selection of approaches, supporting materials, and scaffolds to support students' gradual development of both literacy and test-taking abilities;
- Supporting and respecting students' past life and test-taking experiences, including being patient and empathetic to students' anxiety; and
- Maintaining meaningful instruction by selecting authentic texts and teaching skills relevant to literacy uses outside the classroom (Giouroukakis & Honigsfeld, 2010).

These practices are, of course, essential for all students, but we believe that it is even more important to take care in preparing multilingual students for high-stakes tests. They may have higher levels of anxiety than other students because of past experiences taking tests (both in the United States and in other countries); if they have previously taken standardized tests in the United States, they may have felt frustrated by the linguistic complexity of the test items. Purposeful selection of source texts based in familiar genres and topics can reduce students' anxiety by allowing them to practice test-taking skills without worrying about whether they have completely understood the content of the text.

Preparing Multilingual Students for Standardized Tests

- Teach students how to read and unpack test instructions.

- Teach testing vocabulary, including terminology that is used in instructions and item design.

- Remind students of scoring policies (whether guessing is penalized or appropriate).

- Teach students strategies for addressing different types of test items.

- Give students opportunities to practice under test-like conditions, including with permitted accommodations and using realistic answer sheets

- Review test day procedures, including timing and break policies.

- Encourage students to get a good night's sleep and eat breakfast before the test day.

(Coombe, Folse, & Hubley, 2007)

Timed and On-Demand Writing as a Genre

Teaching students to write under the time constraints of externally mandated tasks can be done using the same approaches as those used in genre-based instruction for other writing assignments. With SFL tools for making sense of complex sentences, students can learn how to analyze a writing task and rubric criteria for what they are required to do and how they should do it. For example, Talia selected a task from the CAHSEE and parsed it into the same graphic organizer (Figure 6.2) the class had used earlier in the year to analyze reading texts (see Figure 2.2).

Figure 6.2. Student analysis of a writing task.

	Connector	Participant	Process	Participant	Circumstances
1	In the story "The Hiking Trip,"	the reader	learns		about the main character, Jeff.
2		Jeff's personality and emotions	are revealed		through the actions and dialogue presented in the story.
3			**Write**	**an essay**	
4	in which	you	**describe**	**the personality and emotions**	**of Jeff**, the main character.
5	How do	*his personal char-acteristics*	*add*		to the events in the story?
6	How does	*the author*	*reveal*	this information	about Jeff in the story?
7			**Use**	**details and examples**	**from the story**
8			to support	your ideas.	

This task is similar to many writing tasks students might encounter on a standardized test. The first two sentences provide background information that orients students to the focus of the task, which in this case is the personality of the main character, Jeff. Using this functional language analysis, students can see that the actual task they must perform is in the third sentence, which starts with an imperative (there is no participant subject, just a process verb) directing them to *write an essay*, and continues with a clause describing what they should do in their essay: describe Jeff's personality and emotions. The two questions (clauses 4 and 5) give students more information about what they should discuss in their essays and how they might structure the response: first an examination of what Jeff's personal characteristics are and how they add to the narrative, followed by an analysis of how the author reveals those characteristics. The final sentence (clauses 7 and 8) is another imperative that directs students to use details and examples in support of their claims. By parsing the task commands into the functions of each portion of the sentence and then identifying which parts are mandatory (imperative verb processes as commands, indicated in bold here) and which are recommendations (the questions in between the two imperative sentences, indicated in italics here), students can figure out what they should focus on in their essays and how they can

structure their essays to maximize their scores on the rubric. When she first introduced students to this test task analysis process, Talia included a vocabulary lesson
on the terminology used to give instructions for exam
tasks.

Just as they do in genre study of real-world
texts throughout the school year, students can learn
to study model essays written in response to sample
exam tasks. Most state testing websites provide
sample essays scored at different levels of success with
explanations of why the essays received their scores.
Analyzing model essays alongside the scoring rubric
(also provided on the state's testing website) will give
students a better understanding of how the criteria
on the rubric relate to the tasks on the prompt and
scores on sample essays. Students can also examine
model essays (exemplars) to determine genre features
that align with what they have learned in class, such
as register choices and imagined audience (knowing
that the real readers will be the exam scorers). As we
noted earlier, exam scoring tends to reward formulaic rather than creative writing, but students can see
from models that it's possible to write passing essays in a few different ways.

> Our experience of scoring students' writing
> with groups of teachers has shown us that
> while voice, as a trait of writing, is rarely
> present on the rubrics of standardized writing
> tasks, it's one of the traits that teachers scoring
> the writing will notice. In Chapter 4, we saw
> Gary work with his students to understand
> and create voice in their writing. Gary's work
> represents the notion that compelling aspects
> of teaching and learning, like voice in writing,
> should not be ignored, because they are
> important for real-world writing. Regardless
> of whether they show up on standardized
> rubrics, they are noticeable to the scorers of
> standardized writing tasks.

While studying the genre of timed and on-demand essays, students can also
learn how to manage their writing process to accomplish the required task most
efficiently. Many of the same process techniques they use in other writing activities can be adapted to work under time pressure. Brainstorming and outlining, for
example, can be helpful as long as students know to just jot down quick notes and
feel comfortable writing from these first ideas rather than exploring multiple possibilities. Karen Russikoff (2013) suggests the mnemonic FRIEDs[13] to help writers
come up with a range of appropriate examples and supporting details:

Facts: true or proven information

Reasons: explanations for why the information supports their point

Incidents: a brief narrative of something that happened that can support the
point

Examples: specific details that illustrate the point

Details: adjectives and adverbs that make the incidents and examples more
specific

By quickly listing a few points for each letter, FRIEDs can give student writers
enough specific detail to jump into writing their essays. In response to tasks that

ask for details from a particular text, students can focus on choosing appropriate facts, reasons, details, incidents, and examples from the story to support their claim.

With their examples chosen, students can then draft a thesis or focus statement that addresses the main requirement of the task, drawing phrases from the wording of the task itself. In the previous example, the thesis might be: *Jeff's personality and emotions show that he has a _____ character.* If students have had practice completing sentence frames for writing thesis statements in other classes, they can use their knowledge of how those sentences are structured to write their own frames based on the task and fill in the blank with an adjective or two drawn from the examples they have selected. An unconventional but useful suggestion to help multilingual writers deal with the time constraints of standardized tests is to write a conclusion sentence that follows a form similar to the thesis immediately after writing the thesis. Although rubrics for timed writing rarely focus on concluding paragraphs, a single concluding sentence can make an essay seem more complete. Students can therefore write a conclusion at the bottom of the last page and then fill in their reasons and examples with the remaining time.

Time management strategies are essential to success on writing exams. Unlike in the day-to-day classroom environment, students need to understand that they should focus on writing about what they already know rather than taking risks. This is true for both content and language: several simpler but accurate sentences will count for more than one complex but error-laden sentence. In organizing an on-demand essay, students should start with their strongest point and plan to include the weakest point last in case they run out of time to go into detail on all points. They should plan to leave a few minutes at the end of the time period for reading through their essay and correcting potentially careless errors, rather than writing up to the last minute. Finally, and most important, students should have multiple opportunities in class to write collaboratively and without time pressure the types of texts that will be tested, and then to practice producing these types of texts on their own under time pressure.

While these test-taking strategies are equally useful to all students, multilingual students often need more explicit instruction in taking US-style multiple-choice and performance tests, as the formats and procedures are not the same worldwide. They also need more instruction in the language of the test, since terminology used in test instructions and in question formats can be confusing. Having multiple opportunities to practice taking tests integrated into their day-to-day learning about genres can reduce students' anxiety by helping them understand how they can use the same linguistic and text analysis skills to make sense of new tasks and readings under limited time.

Rachel, Gary, and Talia Prepare Students for Tests

The teachers in Chapters 3, 4, and 5 of this book, Rachel, Gary, and Talia, used a variety of the approaches described in this chapter to help their ELLs unpack reading and writing tasks and respond effectively to on-demand tasks. The flexible genre-based instructional approach was a way to bring the language into focus in an on-demand writing task or other type of standardized test question. There was no difference in their instructional approach when analyzing texts for language demands and supporting their students in analyzing a test question or writing task as a genre in itself. This way, the students had been engaging in these text analysis activities from the beginning of the year, and when test time arrived in late spring, there was no need for the teachers to shift their emphasis or "drop everything and teach the test." Instead, the process for analyzing texts, tasks, and rubric criteria for their purposes, audience, context, etc. was already a core part of the regular curriculum. For example, Rachel, Gary, and Talia collaborated to locate a variety of on-demand writing tasks from the item banks associated with the Smarter Balanced and the PARCC tests. They selected one hundred items to use with their students. They then broke the items into sets of approximately thirty, aligned to the CCSS reading, writing, and language standards.

The teachers engaged their students in a process of text analysis that included unpacking the language of each task by answering some of these questions:

1. What is this question asking me to do?
2. Is there a text type or genre associated with what this question is asking me to do? For example, is the question asking me to argue, explain, or recount?
3. How do I know that? (What specific language tells me this?)
4. To whom am I writing?
5. Am I supposed to remain objective and inform or take a position and persuade?
6. Does this question refer me to a text?
7. What evidence from a text or set of texts should I use to support my response?

Beginning with this list, the teachers designed a variety of questions to fit the specific items they had chosen to analyze. Additionally, they designed some categorizing lessons in which students sorted test items based on a variety of criteria. The teachers gave students the items on strips of paper so they could be handled easily and sorted in columns on the desks and tables according to the following categories:

- Questions that ask me to *make an argument or take a position* on an issue
- Questions that ask me to *objectively explain* more than one side of an issue

- Questions that ask me to *reflect on or recount a personal experience*
- Questions that require specific *evidence from texts* provided
- Questions that ask me to *draw from my own personal experiences*

In these two activities, students were not asked to respond to the tasks or to locate any particular answer; the idea was instead to analyze and sort the tasks into genre categories that could be unpacked with these and other questions.

Once students had categorized the tasks according to purpose, they listed common language used by test designers when writing a particular type of task. For example, some of the verb phrases used in an item that asks students to take a position may include *take a side, state your claim, argue for or against*, and *take a position*. The teachers posted reference charts around their classrooms with lists of the language used in different kinds of tasks as a resource for students in the next steps of the process. These next steps involved figuring out how to respond to a task once they had determined what it was asking them to do. It's important to note that unpacking tasks and determining what each task requires are such critical steps that you can spend a lot of time on them without having students also practice writing responses so long as students are already engaged in other regular writing experiences.

Rachel, Gary, and Talia designed opportunities for their students to practice planning their writing by engaging them in task analysis and collaborative outlining. The students shared their outlines with the class, discussing the goals of the task, sharing the ways they had decoded the language of the task, and illustrating how they decided to respond to the task. This approach emphasized awareness of the language, goals, and purposes of the task, as opposed to focusing their energy on the written response. Similar approaches could be employed from the beginning of the year and on through the testing season; as long as they support students in developing metalinguistic awareness, the approaches are beneficial to students for a variety of academic purposes, including their performances on high-stakes tests.

This chapter demonstrates ways that we as teachers can maintain our accountability to our students with equitable literacy instruction even in the face of high-stakes standardized tests. The next chapter adds to ideas of how to share the work you are doing with ELLs with parents, other people at the school, and the larger community.

Reaching Outward: Accountability through Advocating for ELLs

As students become active and frequent readers, performance on standardized reading tests increases. . . . Students who become lifelong readers and writers become lifelong learners. This is a better predictor of academic success than any test results.

—Ada & Campoy, 2004, p. 40

W ithin the noun *accountability* is the verb *account*, which means "to furnish a justifying analysis or explanation" (*Merriam-Webster's*). Throughout this book, we have emphasized the importance of being accountable to our students in the form of linguistically responsible teaching that prepares them for using literacy in the real world. As we noted in Chapter 1, however, accountability in contemporary American education generally refers more to using test scores to demonstrate students' academic performance. Here in our final chapter, we argue that as teachers we do have a responsibility to communicate about our teaching and our students' learning to people outside our classrooms—but that test scores are not the best way to do so. Instead, the language and literacy work that our English language learner students produce during language-focused GBI lessons can provide far more informative and meaningful evidence of their learning as well as of their preparation for using literacy beyond the classroom. This chapter builds on the classroom principles discussed in earlier chapters to show you how you can communicate your approach to accountability to stakeholders outside the classroom.

Accountability to the School Community

The most immediate people outside of our individual classrooms with a stake in ELL students' learning are our colleagues and administrators within our schools and districts. In middle and high school, multilingual students have contact with dozens of different teachers, administrators, and school staff during the academic year. While we feel that all of these people *should* know more about who students are, we also understand that it can be difficult for each of them to get to know hundreds of students with the degree of personal knowledge that classroom teachers can have. Therefore, we hope that you, as the students' teacher, will be an advocate for the literacy work your multilingual students are doing in your classroom throughout the year.

Working with the ESL Specialist

If you are an ELA teacher whose school or district has ESL specialists, coaches, or resource teachers with whom you can collaborate, we highly recommend working closely with them. Through regular communication and discussion of multilingual students (both those who are still ELL-designated and those who have been reclassified but still need support developing their academic English), you can share your understanding of individual students' growth, strengths, and learning needs, as well as strategies for scaffolding and accommodating instruction and assessment. This knowledge can also be valuable to share with your students' other teachers, who may not know as much about their literacy abilities or about how to accommodate and scaffold their work. As we reviewed in Chapter 6, multilingual students have widely differing first language and English literacy backgrounds, meaning that they can't all be supported with the same accommodations for assignments and tests. In collaboration with the ESL specialist, you can work with colleagues in English and other departments who teach the same groups of students to develop common accommodations for ELLs, including these practices:

- Know which students are literate in their home languages and can benefit from using dictionaries or writing notes in their first languages.
- Know which students are fluent English speakers but struggle with literacy and could benefit from scaffolds that allow them to talk through ideas before writing them down.

- Share graphic organizers and metalanguage terminology so other teachers can support students in learning to read and write the genres of their disciplines (lab reports, history analysis papers, etc.).

These collaborative discussions can also lead to developing shared norms for appropriate accommodations for multilingual students on formal tests. As we noted earlier, not all ELL students have the same degree of home language literacy, so only some will benefit from using bilingual glossaries or dictionaries as they take tests. Some may need extra time as a primary accommodation, while others may need additional supports. ESL resource teachers should be able to recommend accommodations that will allow all multilingual students to show their content knowledge. When students receive consistent accommodations from all their teachers, they can better build their overall ability to demonstrate their literacy skills. The ESL specialist can help with writing rubrics that separate language proficiency from other aspects of writing knowledge, allowing ELLs to show what they *do* know about writing as well as how their language knowledge is developing.

ESL specialists can help classroom teachers throughout their curriculum planning work. One way they can help is to develop lesson modifications that increase ELLs' opportunity to learn the academic language and content that will be on assessments (and that is needed for success in school more generally). ESL resource teachers may co-teach lessons, demonstrating techniques for eliciting students' understanding and facilitating deeper engagement with course content through multiple modalities. After multilingual students take tests (both classroom and standardized), classroom teachers can meet with the ESL specialist to analyze the test results. The ESL specialist can bring knowledge of second language learning and development as well as of students' language proficiency into the conversation, especially when discussing placement and ongoing assessment results.

Working with Other Teachers and Administrators

Collaboration with colleagues in other departments and with resource teachers is essential to working toward accountability to our multilingual students, but we also need to demonstrate to administrators what we are doing. As teachers we need to show how we are supporting our multilingual students' learning through accountability to the standards and district expectations. Teachers who work with multilingual students can report regularly (monthly or more often) to the English department chair and school administrators about ELL students' progress. While this may be represented in part through charting test scores, GBI provides us with myriad other materials to show qualitatively how much more the students are learning. This is a place where portfolios of student work can be used as evidence of ELLs' development and of their ability to use language and literacy in real-world

Reports about ELL students' successes should not be limited to teachers and administrators. Everyone in a school site, including paraprofessionals and custodial staff, shares in the success of all students and should be invited to attend celebrations of student successes. At one school site, for example, the lunch staff, custodial staff, campus security, administrative assistants, and paraprofessionals were included in any communication about student achievement and were always invited to attend every celebration. Very often, many of them came; after all, they were part of the school community and some had children enrolled in the school; as such, they had a stake in the success of all students.

contexts. Administrators will, of course, also be concerned with what we are doing to ensure students' success on high-stakes assessments, so it's important also to discuss accommodations and scaffolds that seem to be working (and those that are not working) for individual students. As described in Chapter 6, it may also be worth discussing how we're explicitly preparing students for year-end standardized tests through analysis of assessment tasks and prompts, for example, or gradual removal of scaffolds in practice assessment activities.

At administrative levels above our individual schools, it's difficult to provide this kind of personalized reporting. District and state administrators will most likely only see ELL students' test scores and graduation rates, making it all the more important to develop advocates among the school-level administrators who meet with district officials. Teachers can, however, make ELL students' progress more visible through community outreach, as we discuss later in this chapter. When district and state administrators are able to draw on these contributions to bolster publication of test scores, ELL students may be able to avoid being categorized as failures in the public eye. Table 7.1 revisits the chart that we shared in Chapter 1, summarizing some of the approaches we have discussed throughout this book with respect to what activities demonstrate student learning to the various stakeholders in the school and community.

Talking with Parents

Parents are concerned with their children's progress and learning. Cultural differences in views on appropriate interaction with school personnel, however, means that immigrant parents may not reach out to ask teachers how their kids are doing. Linguistically, they may not feel comfortable talking with teachers in English, either. Parents may know that their children are preparing to take some kind of tests but not what the tests entail. Others may have bad memories from their own experiences taking standardized tests as children. Depending on how high-stakes tests were conducted in their home countries, parents may feel that teachers should be doing more—or that teachers are doing too much—to prepare students for exams. They may also not be aware of the many other forms of assessment you are

Table 7.1. Summary of Ways to Be Accountable to Stakeholders

Accountability to whom?	Demonstrated through . . .
Students	· Valuing language diversity as an asset and resource · Real-world literacy practices · Preparing for college and career · Focusing on genres of school and life · Teaching how to take tests (show what they already know) · Culturally diverse and respectful texts
School (teachers and administrators)	· Preparing ELLs for literacy in subject areas · Identifying and addressing language demands, setting language objectives, and providing relevant and targeted language supports · Developing shared metalanguage for talking about language within genres across subject areas and grade levels · Discussing ELL students' test results and planning scaffolds and accommodations
District and state	· Test scores · Other formal assessments · College and career readiness
Community (and parents)	· Showing language and content knowledge growth · Showing that ELLs can do more than take tests · Emphasizing progress and growth · Inviting families to learn about assessment policy and how to support students

doing in the classroom. Alternatively, many immigrant parents highly respect the teaching profession and may feel that their own ideas on their children's schooling aren't relevant.

Talking with Parents about Students' Progress

Teachers should aim to maintain regular communication with parents and guardians throughout the academic year. By keeping parents updated on their children's progress, you can help them understand how assessment processes work and which forms of assessment hold high stakes for their children. Many schools now have electronic gradebooks that are available online to parents and guardians, but these can pose some problems for parents of immigrant multilingual youth. One, of course, is the language barrier: if all the information is in English, parents may not be able to understand what is written. More important, however, is the way that online gradebooks usually just report scores on assignments without

How many parents of your current students have you met? How did you meet them? How many were parents of multilingual students? What were their concerns about their children's school performance? Does your school have translation services to support meetings with parents who don't speak English well? Does your site have an English learner advisory committee (ELAC) or other committee that regularly discusses issues related to multilingual learners? If so, who is on this committee?

situating them in any kind of context. Parents may misunderstand the degree of importance an assignment has. A solution to this problem that can benefit both our students and their families is to create a website with descriptions of course goals and explanations of individual assignments. L1-literate multilingual students could offer their skills to translate the website into their home languages, thus increasing both their own understanding of what they are expected to do and their parents' understanding of the class. Assignments can be accompanied by timelines indicating when parts are due and when scores will be posted. Table 7.2 recommends timing for reporting various forms of assignments and assessments to families and administrators.

Teachers may wish to send home a monthly update to keep parents informed about their children's progress. These could be in the form of a printed newsletter with translations if needed or phone calls with the assistance of an interpreter. Such updates could also address upcoming high-stakes assignments, letting parents know what they can do to help their children at home, as well as when they shouldn't push students to study (such as for English language proficiency tests). While in some situations students can serve as interpreters and cultural brokers in

Table 7.2. Timeline for Communicating with Families and Administrators[14]

Assessment	Description	Frequency	Feedback
Classwork and homework	Activities completed in class and at home	Daily collection, weekly review	Simple corrections given to students and scores reported to parents in online grade-book
Journal	Ongoing informal writing assignments	Weekly	Written feedback to students each week; shared with parents monthly
GBI writing assignments	Extended, multidraft texts in genres under study	Monthly	Written feedback and rubric-based score; returned to students and sent home to parents
Portfolio	Collection of student's best work with written reflections	Quarterly	Written feedback and rubric-based score each quarter; parents and administrators invited to annual Portfolio Day
Practice standardized tests	Format and content of annual assessments	Quarterly	Results explained in a memo (in English and families' home languages) sent home to parents and presented to administrators

communications with their parents, you need to be sensitive to what is appropriate or inappropriate for youth to be responsible for and to call on available interpretation and translation services (from the school district or other adult volunteers) as needed. As much as possible, this should take the form of two-way communication, in which you listen to parents' concerns as much as you share your own with the families. In parent-teacher conferences, teachers have found success starting with an opportunity for immigrant parents to voice their concerns and ask the teacher questions prior to the teacher's report on the child's progress (Levine & Bunch, 2007).

Community organizations can be helpful for making culturally appropriate connections with parents, who might be uncomfortable talking face-to-face with teachers on their own. Other parents may not be able to read in their home language or in English and need support from adults who speak their home language. Schools have found that home visits, in which teachers check in with families at their places of residence, can be beneficial in building parents' trust of the teachers, as long as teachers are able to process their experience without a deficit view of the families' living situations (Levine & Bunch, 2007).

Another asset that should be encouraged in supporting parents' understanding of their children's performance at school are school-based parent organizations. Although for cultural or linguistic reasons many immigrant parents will feel uncomfortable participating in the mainstream PTA, they may find benefit in joining with other immigrant parents in a formal or informal group. Many school districts have something like California's official English Learner Advisory Committees,[15] which consist of parents, community members, teachers, and school administrators concerned about multilingual students' academic performance. This group might meet quarterly or more often and discusses curriculum and assessment of ELL students. In cases where there are many parents from the same language or cultural background, parents might want to form a group specifically concerned with their own children's experiences.

Hosting a bilingual family night during the first semester can encourage parents to feel comfortable visiting the school and can show them what their children are learning. Teachers at one local school, for example, held a family writing night and invited parents to come with all their children, not just those enrolled at the school. They set up the school's multipurpose room with exhibits of the students' finished writing on bulletin boards and laid out examples of the books and articles the students were reading during class. After the families had had time to walk around the room admiring their children's writing and had picked up snacks from a table at the back of the room, the teachers projected pictures from a short story about a middle school student celebrating a traditional holiday in his family; they read the story aloud in English and encouraged the students to translate for parents who didn't speak English. They then distributed to each family packets with writing paper and space for pictures. Parents and children were asked to talk with each other about a particular tradition in their family and then to write a story telling about that tradition. As much as possible, they were encouraged to write bilingually, in both the parents' language and in English, so the stories could serve as a resource for future students with the same home language. Younger brothers and sisters could draw the pictures, while older siblings often served as translators or as experts in how to explain the celebration. After the families had finished their books, the teachers photocopied them to keep for other students to read and bound the originals with the spiral binding machine so the families could take their bilingual books home.

Teachers can also integrate other ways of showing parents how their children are doing on day-to-day assignments. Portfolios can be used to document progress throughout the year. These are especially powerful if students are given some choice of which assignments to include, selecting based on those they feel best show their own learning and growth. Students can track their performance on practice tests and other preparatory assignments in a portfolio and then write cover letters to their parents in the family's home language explaining what the test scores show about their learning. Portfolios can be brought out during parent-teacher conferences and passed on to the following year's teachers if appropriate. These portfolios could also be displayed at a year-end celebration of students' achievements to which parents are invited. Involving parents in this process through regular conferencing, with the student present, is a positive way to keep parents apprised of students' specific growth and target areas.

In another school we have visited, the teachers organize an annual Portfolio Day in late spring. The portfolios are developed from the beginning of the school year and consist of a binder with sections for each school subject. In each section, students select their best work and write reflections on how this

Setting Up a Bilingual Family Night

• Provide food (light snacks and refreshments) and child care so parents don't have to worry about their other children.

• Include translators who can speak the languages of the families that come.

• Use the time to show off the students' work and the curriculum rather than telling parents about it. Parents can participate in a gallery walk of their children's school writing, and students can stand by their work to explain in their home languages what they have written.

• Engage the parents and their children in a fun activity in which parents can see how much their children are learning and can also share their own knowledge. Families could create a bilingual book, with text written in their home language and/or English and illustrations drawn by the children. Topics might include family traditions, holiday customs from their home countries, or folktales. Building on the genre study the students have done in class, students could introduce their parents to a new genre as well.

• See Robertson (2007) for more suggestions.

work illustrates their growth in that subject. By Portfolio Day, students have collected at least six work samples showing growth in all subject areas. They dress up for the occasion and stand before their peers to present their academic growth. All students participate, and grading is based on effort more than academic achievement. Through Portfolio Day, the multilingual students are able to highlight the progress they have made in both their language development and their ability to write in multiple genres of academic texts. A widely recognized community event, Portfolio Day often includes parents and other community members. Because their children are there to explain their own portfolios, parents have access to the information. Multilingual students can be supported in writing portfolio introductions or reflections in their home languages to further help their parents see what they have learned.

Talking with Parents about High-Stakes Tests

Standardized tests as they are used in US schools are a particularly American concern that can be perceived by immigrant parents in different ways depending on their own previous experiences with testing in their home countries. Some parents may feel that they need to pressure their children to study more, while others may dismiss the importance of adequate rest and nutrition on testing days.

Standardized tests can have very different meanings in other cultures, which may lead parents to put unnecessary pressure on their children during annual testing. A survey of how high-stakes tests are used around the globe reveals some extreme differences that help explain parents' possible misunderstanding. The sidebar on page 140 shows examples of ways that tests are used in other countries and how they may have much more extreme consequences for children in those countries than their US counterparts. Parents from China or India, for example, might not realize that the annual standardized tests in the United States have little impact on their children's futures, whereas parents from Brazil may not support their children enough to prepare for high-stakes high school exit exams.

To better prepare parents for supporting their children during high-stakes assessment, school- or community-based parent groups can organize workshops for parents to discuss what the testing policies are, what the associated stakes are for their children and the school, and how parents can support their children to perform their best on the tests. Some of the questions worth addressing are as follows:

- What are the tests your children have to take?
- Why do they have to take these tests?
- What accommodations can be provided to support ELL students?
- What are the consequences of the tests?
- What rights do multilingual families have with respect to services?

High-Stakes Tests in Other Countries

- *As gatekeeper to high school*: In many countries, high school isn't a guarantee or requirement. For example, in many countries in Africa, a low score on the secondary school entrance exam means that a student's academic career is over unless parents can pay for the student to retake the exam the following year.

- *Sorting students into tracked high schools*: In other countries, students' test results determine what kind of high school they can attend and therefore what their academic and professional future is. In Mexico, for example, test scores determine whether a child will attend a vocational or an academic high school; without an academic high school education, it's much more difficult for the student to go on to university. Similarly, in India, tenth graders take a test that determines their course of study (science, arts, or commerce) for the rest of high school.

- *University admissions*: Many countries have a national exam that is used for university admissions, often as the sole factor (unlike US colleges, which consider high school GPA, essays, recommendation letters, and extracurricular activities as well). Also unlike United States, many countries only allow students to take the exam for a single university; if they aren't accepted to that university, they have to wait until the following year to retake the exam for the same or a different university. The university entrance test may also determine the student's major or how much scholarship money she or he can receive. Furthermore, in Uzbekistan, for example, as in some other countries, it's rare for a student to begin university more than a year after finishing high school, and there are few alternative pathways to four-year universities, so there's extra pressure for students to do well on the entrance exam for their chosen university.

- *Test-prep cram schools*: In Japan and South Korea, secondary school and university entrance exams are such high priority that families will invest vast amounts of money in after-school programs that promise to raise their children's test scores. These programs often run for four to six hours daily (after the regular school day), with much of the instruction strictly focused on learning how to take the tests.

- *Test scores as identity*: In China, secondary school and university entrance exam test scores become associated with people's core identity. As a colleague explained, "High-stakes testing in China determines a person's fate and life in adulthood. It is the most important thing for a child to go through at all levels of education. High school is the most intensified time."

- *Parental pressure*: How much pressure parents place on their children to study for high school and university exams varies widely across the globe. In South and East Asia, parents are highly involved in making sure their children study for tests. Teenagers in South Korea and Nepal, among other countries, may commit suicide when they receive unfavorable results because of the shame of letting their families down. Parents in Europe, Latin America, and Africa, in contrast, seem less concerned with pressuring their children to study, even when the tests carry lifelong consequences.

Teachers can participate in these workshops, explaining how they are helping students learn academic language and prepare for the tests and showing parents how their instruction has helped students to develop the literacy and language skills they need to do their best on the tests, but also stressing that instruction is helping them learn to use English in the real world as well. Show examples of the kinds of exams and other assessments (such as benchmark tests or writing portfolios) that are used in the district. If possible, provide translations so that parents can see the format of tasks and the types of questions asked. A later meeting can address how to interpret students' scores on high-stakes tests so that parents can understand what they mean with respect to their children's progress. Schools will need to have translation services for these meetings or at least provide a handout in the parents' languages. The sidebar on page 142 offers a brief list of pointers for parents, with translations in Russian, Spanish, and Chinese.

Accountability to the Larger Community

We now turn to how the detailed principles in this book relate to issues of accountability to the school, district, and community, suggesting ways that classroom teachers and principals can show that the ELLs at their school are learning, even if their test scores aren't as high as those of non-ELLs. Genre-based instruction by its very nature leads to the creation of texts that can (and should) be shared with wider audiences; you can help frame the presentation of the work so that the community understands how it illustrates your ELL students' strengths and growth.

One of the goals behind the standards movement of the 1990s and 2000s was to hold schools accountable to the community for students' learning (TESOL, 2013). Standardized tests were intended to show where students were doing well and where they were not—so that the public could support schools that did well and demand change at those that did not. In recent years, newspapers have published school scores on year-end standardized tests, leading to editorials about how poorly schools are doing or how teachers should be better preparing students for the tests. The problem, however, is that too often the public accepts test scores as being neutral, objective measures of students' performance (Shohamy, 2006). People are generally unaware of the factors we outlined in Chapter 6 that make most standardized tests invalid measures of the abilities of many students, particularly of English language learners (Casanave, 2004). School administrators need to be able to explain test scores to the public in ways that interpret the results accurately while also discussing the purposes and uses of the test scores (Solórzano, 2008). Without this interpretation, the general public may wrongly believe that multilingual students are at fault for bringing down their school's scores.

What Can Parents Do to Help Their Children Prepare for Tests?

- Help your children understand why they are being tested.
- Do not stress performance on any one test as evidence of your children's abilities.
- Provide a quiet area at home for doing homework.
- Encourage your children to read and write in both your home language and English.
- Bring home magazines and newspapers in your home language and English to give your children something to read at home.
- Ask about what your children are doing in classes at school.

Russian:

Что могут сделать делать родители, чтобы помочь своим детям подготовиться к экзамеам?
- Помогите своим детям понять, почему они сдают экзамены.
- Не рассматривайте успеваемость на любом экзамене в качестве доказательства способностей своих детей.
- Найдите дома удобное место для выполнения домашних заданий.
- Поощряйте своих детей читать и писать как по-русски, так и по-английски.
- Приносите домой журналы и газеты и на родном языке и на английском, чтобы дать своим детям возможность читать дома.
- Спросите о том, что ваши дети делают на занятиях в школе.

Spanish:

¿Qué pueden hacer los padres para ayudar a sus hijos a prepararse?
- Ayude a sus hijos a comprender por qué deben tomar pruebas estandarizadas.
- No ponga más importancia en el rendimiento de una prueba u otra como evidencia de las habilidades de sus hijos.
- Proporcionar una zona tranquila en la casa para hacer la tarea.
- Anime a sus hijos a leer y escribir tanto en su idioma natal como en inglés.
- Traiga revistas y periódicos tanto en su idioma natal como en inglés para dar a sus hijos algo para leer en casa.
- Pregunte acerca de las actividades que sus hijos realizan en las clases en la escuela.

Chinese:

家长们可以怎样帮助孩子准备？
- 帮助您的孩子理解为什么他们需要接受测试；
- 不要把任何一个测试结果作为评判您的孩子的能力的证据；
- 在家里为孩子提供一个安静的做作业的区域；
- 鼓励孩子用与家人交流的语言和英语进行阅读和写作；
- 把用您在家中所使用的语言编写的报刊杂志和英语报刊杂志带回家给孩子阅读；
- 询问您的孩子在学校的课堂里做了什么。

Administrators can ensure that publicity gives voice to the ELLs and their teachers when school test scores are reported publicly. One way is through showing that ELLs are making progress, both by documenting growth on standardized tests across the years (especially how individual students have improved, rather than just an overall number of all ELL scores) and by showing all the other ways that ELLs are succeeding in school. Schools might wish to host online or in-person events where the community can check out ePortfolios and galleries of students' work with annotations to show how they have improved, emphasizing growth even if the work still has errors. The Portfolio Day described earlier, for example, is the culmination of a full year of developing writing and consistent reflection throughout the process.

GBI also facilitates highlighting other ways that students are learning. Students can demonstrate to the community what they can do with English through public performances, writing letters to the editor of the local newspaper, or testifying at city council or school board meetings. These actions don't have to be separate from their regular classroom activities, either. Just as Talia's students analyzed book and movie reviews in order to write their own, multilingual students can examine how editorial columns and letters to the editor use language to convey a particular perspective on an issue. If they are working on synthesis of multiple texts, they might read reports from various perspectives about standardized testing in their community and respond with stories of their own progress.

As we wrap up this book, we want to present one final area of accountability that is essential to teachers' effective work with multilingual students: accountability to ourselves. We believe that as professionals, teachers owe it to themselves to continue to develop knowledge of how language works in the content areas as well as how to teach language in ways that help ELLs and other students learn and show what they have learned.

Teacher Professional Development

Although this book is not specifically about professional development models, we do argue that ongoing professional development that includes some element of practice-based teacher learning is an essential aspect of accountability to ELLs. The teachers showcased in this book, Rachel, Gary, and Talia, participated in a practice-based professional development model called "lesson study" along with two other teachers, Laura and Elizabeth. Lesson study is a popular and effective form of practice-based teacher professional development that is common in Japan and is gaining popularity in the United States as well (Lewis, 2002; Lewis, Perry, Friedkin, & Roth, 2012). In the lesson study that formed the backdrop for this book, these five teachers collaboratively selected topics centered on writing.

They researched and planned lessons, observed one teacher from the group teach the lessons, and analyzed student learning. Together, they used their analysis of the teaching and learning to inform their next steps (Pella, 2015b). Rachel, Gary, Talia, Laura, and Elizabeth all agreed that lesson study was an effective model for developing their language and literacy pedagogies (Pella, 2011, 2015a).

In Chapters 3 through 5, we showed how Rachel, Gary, and Talia taught language-focused, genre-based lessons in their individual classrooms. It's important to underscore that these teachers didn't go it alone. They developed, tested, and refined their language teaching collaboratively across three years and nine cycles of lesson study. Furthermore, throughout the lesson study process, the teachers collected and collaboratively analyzed data from student learning and improved their own formative assessment practices. Some of the data they collected included observation notes and informal recording of student responses and interactions (through running records, checklists, note taking, and sometimes audio or video recording), as well as various artifacts and texts their students produced from the lessons. The collaborative analysis of data provided information about how students were progressing in each lesson. This process also had another benefit: the teachers learned how to collect and interpret data to demonstrate the growth and progress of their students (Pella, 2012). As we discussed earlier, capturing and describing ELLs' progress is a key consideration for celebrating the learning of students who may not perform well on tests but are progressing in other ways.

Lesson study is just one of many types of practice-based teacher professional development models. The term *practice-based* for the purposes of this book means that there are structures and processes in place for teacher learning to occur in real time, in real classroom contexts with real students, who also benefit from the high-quality learning experiences their teachers design, test, and refine after careful text selection and collaborative planning (O'Hara, Pritchard, Huang, & Pella, 2013a, 2013b). In addition to lesson study teams, some other popular practice-based teacher professional development models include teacher learning lab teams, collaborative inquiry groups, coaching cycles, book study and research study groups, school-based professional learning communities, peer observation teams, instructional rounds, individual practitioner inquiry, and collaborative action research groups.

Practice-based, research-supported learning models offer an alternative to the most common form of teacher professional development in the United States: the top-down transmission model, which has been critiqued for its reliance on didactic information transfer techniques (Fernandez & Chokshi, 2002). Many teachers can relate to the notion that American "factory-model schools" offer little time for teachers to spend working together to develop curricula, plan lessons, discuss teaching strategies, or assess student work in authentic ways (Darling-Hammond, 2006). In this system, teachers don't have a way to harvest their collective experiences, share common concerns, and systematically integrate and refine their knowledge (Chokshi & Fernandez, 2004).

Research shows that teacher collaboration and some element of practice-based learning are essential to teacher professional development (Darling-Hammond, Wei, Andree, Richardson, & Orphanos, 2009; Marrongelle, Sztajn, & Smith, 2013; Pella, 2015a, 2015b). Our focus in this book has been to highlight several classrooms where the teachers demonstrated language pedagogies developed through their lesson study participation that both supported and challenged the language and literacy learning of their ELLs. Rachel, Gary, and Talia had partici-

- What kinds of professional development have you encountered that might connect to working with ELLs?

- Which have been the most effective for you?

- What types of practice-based professional learning might you design in collaboration with others?

- Does your school provide a structured time in your school day or week to collaborate with other teachers? If not, how might you advocate for such time?

pated in other externally designed professional development sessions that they had found worthwhile, but it wasn't until they tried out *in practice* some of what they had learned that they were able to truly operationalize some of the language and literacy practices advocated in those sessions.

Conclusion

We've now reached the end of our journey through assessment and accountability issues in teaching multilingual learners. We hope you've learned from the stories we've told of Rachel's, Talia's, and Gary's classrooms, demonstrating how mainstream English teachers with little additional training in second language development were able to support their ELL students in learning both the academic language and the genres they needed to succeed in school and beyond. What the teachers did was situated well within the scope of their schools' curriculum plans and the state standards, but rather than rely solely on materials provided by textbook publishers, they sought out real-world texts that gave their students a sense of how the genres they were studying varied as they were used for communicative purposes. They found support for these endeavors in their practice-based professional development with the lesson study group, which provided them with ongoing resources and feedback on their teaching.

As we wrap up this book, we want to talk about where *you* can begin supporting the multilingual students in your classroom. The following suggestions require some work, on your part and on that of your colleagues, but we feel they will contribute to your students' success. We recommend more of our favorite resources (books and websites) in the annotated bibliography at the end of this book.

1. Learn more about genre-based instruction, particularly as it applies to working with multilingual learners. One book that clearly explains the connections between functional grammar and genre is María Estela Brisk's book *Engaging Students in Academic Literacy* (2015), which presents CCSS-aligned lesson plans and activities for text analysis and writing. Eugenia Mora-Flores's book *Writing Instruction for English Learners: A Focus on Genre* (2008) provides reproducible graphic organizers as well as step-by-step processes for engaging ELL students in genre study. For more about genre-based instruction, though without the specific focus on ELLs, we love Heather Lattimer's book *Thinking through Genre: Units of Study in Reading and Writing Workshops 4–12* (2003).

2. Learn more about SFL tools you can use to help students analyze the language of texts. We recommend Pauline Gibbons's books for this purpose, including the new edition of *Scaffolding Language, Scaffolding Learning* (2015) and *English Learners, Academic Literacy, and Thinking* (2009). Luciana C. de Oliveira and Mary Schleppegrell introduce the concepts of SFL grammar to K–12 teachers in an accessible way in their book *Focus on Grammar and Meaning* (2015). Another useful resource explaining SFL with connections specifically to reading is Zhihui Fang and Mary Schleppegrell's *Reading in Secondary Content Areas* (2008).

3. Learn about your own multilingual students. A good place to start is by reviewing the information your school already has about them, including their English language proficiency scores, their grades and standardized test scores from previous years, and their home language survey information. But then go much further and talk to their past years' teachers, to the ESL teacher or ELL specialist, and, above all else, to the students themselves. While some multilingual students are embarrassed to be identified as language learners in front of the whole class, they may be open to talking with you one to one (if they're more comfortable speaking) or writing a language learning autobiography (if they're more comfortable writing).

4. Learn about the resources available at your school and district for supporting ELLs and their teachers. Talk with the ESL resource specialist to find out what he or she can offer you as support, either materials or personal time, to help your multilingual students catch up with their classmates and demonstrate their learning. Find out if your school or district has an English learner advisory council, and if so, attend the meetings to get to know your students' parents and hear what's going on.

5. Talk with your colleagues (grade level and subject area teams, ESL specialists, and administrators) about policies in place in the district

and school with respect to assessing multilingual students and accommodations they can have on standardized tests. Discuss ways of bringing language instruction into test preparation in all subject areas, including the development of a shared metalanguage for talking about language. Envision ways of sharing alternative displays of students' successes (Portfolio Day, websites, etc.) with the community, particularly if there has been local outcry over standardized test scores.

Returning to NCTE's ELL Brief and the recommendations it makes for working with multilingual students, we want to highlight a key phrase in the section on working with multilingual students in mainstream classrooms: "Bilinguals need three types of knowledge to become literate in a second language. They need to know the second language; they need to know literacy; and they need world knowledge (Bernhardt, 1991)" (p. xi). The approach we have described throughout this book, focused on using linguistic analysis tools of systemic functional linguistics within genre-based instruction, allows students to learn all three: about language, about reading and writing, and about how texts are used in the real world. We invite you to pick up the other books in the Principles in Practice imprint based in the ELL Brief, each of which introduces a different aspect of teaching ELLs, including reading, writing, and community engagement.

We hope that you find value in the tools for language and genre instruction presented here. Maintaining our accountability *to* our multilingual students while also being accountable *for* their performance is an ongoing challenge. Just as Rachel, Gary, and Talia committed themselves to practice-based professional development aimed at building their teaching acumen, we believe this is entirely possible for all teachers to do. Good luck on your future journey!

Appendix: How to Develop Language-Focused Genre-Based Lessons

Prepare

Content Objectives: Determine what you are required to teach in this lesson (by your school or state standards) as well as what you want your students to learn. Some teachers prefer to set both content objectives and literacy objectives. (See how Gary did this in Chapter 5.)

Text Selection: Choose real-world texts by focusing on the genre, the texts' social and communicative purposes, and their relevance to your content and literacy objectives. Seek out accessible and engaging texts that use a variety of text structures toward a shared communicative purpose. (See how Rachel, Gary, and Talia chose texts in Chapters 3, 4, and 5, respectively.)

Assessment Design: Select or write performance tasks that will allow you to determine how well your students are progressing toward your language, literacy, and content objectives. (See how Talia designed a performance task in Chapter 5.)

Language Objectives: Review the content and literacy objectives, the texts you have selected, and the tasks and assessments you have designed to identify language demands (where the language of the texts or the assessments may cause difficulties for your students, particularly for ELLs). Consider what thinking processes students will be asked to do and what language they will need to carry out those processes. Articulate specific language objectives to address the language demands that you will assess in your lessons and unit as a whole. (See the guidelines in Chapter 2 for writing language objectives and the Chapters 3, 4, and 5 Unit Overview tables for sample language objectives.)

Accessibility: Determine what language supports, scaffolds, multimedia, and explicit instruction your students will need in order to access the texts. (See some of the scaffolds Rachel, Gary, and Talia created in Chapters 3, 4, and 5.)

Teach

Deconstruction/Text Analysis: Engage your students in a series of challenge-centered activities in which they investigate how texts are created and how texts vary within a genre. Students should become experts on the essential components of a genre, viewing them through multiple lenses. They can examine the macro structures of texts, as Rachel's students did in Chapter 3, or the language that is used in a genre, as Gary's students did in Chapter 4. Students can teach one another in investigation stations. (See how Rachel set up investigation stations in Chapter 3.) Students should be supported in taking notes on their readings and organizing their notes in a data bank that they can use in future writing tasks, as Talia's students did in Chapter 5.

Writing: Create pathways and scaffolds so that all students are successful at creating texts within the genre of the unit. If the final writing task is in response to a text or a set of texts, present the final writing task to students *before* doing any of the reading. Unpack the language of the task and the criteria that will be used to assess the task. Keep these posted and refer back to them during the unit. Support students to make entries into their data bank that are strategically focused toward building a case for responding to the final writing task. Teacher-led think-alouds can model the writing process, demonstrate how to provide feedback, or illustrate planning for editing. (See how Gary and Talia did this in Chapters 4 and 5.) Jointly construct a text as a whole class so students experience the process with support. (We discuss how Rachel could have done this in Chapter 3.) When students write independently, they should have ample support from comfortable writing groups (see how Gary set up writing groups in Chapter 4) and frequent opportunities to practice giving one another feedback (as both Gary's and Talia's students did in Chapters 4 and 5).

Assess

Formative Assessment: Monitor students' learning throughout the unit, being flexible enough in your planning to make changes to your instruction when you notice students need more or different supports. (See how Talia implemented formative assessment in Chapter 5.)

Summative Assessment: Evaluate students' writing using checklists or rubrics that are familiar to them and that use criteria that have been thoroughly discussed throughout the unit. (See how Talia's class developed criteria in academic language in Chapter 5.)

Standardized Assessment: Prepare students throughout the school year for standardized tests with ongoing activities that engage them in learning and analyzing the language of assessment tasks. Incorporate this instruction with genre-based instruction that analyzes real-world texts so that students recognize the connections between what they are learning in class and the test tasks. (See Chapter 6 for examples of how the teachers prepared their students for standardized tests.)

Reflect and Apply

Consider what the data from formative and summative assessments are showing you about *what* your students have learned (both content and language) as well as *how* they are learning (verbal processing, thinking through confusion, asking questions, problem solving, actively engaging, participating in class discussions, etc.). Use informal data (from talking with and observing your students) along with the more formal data (from student work) to inform your next steps in planning instruction. Whenever possible, collaborate with other teachers and professionals to share ideas and document student growth. Determine shared approaches for your department and school to analyze and communicate students' learning within and beyond the school.

Notes

1. All names of schools, communities, places, and people are pseudonyms. Some of the people are composite descriptions, pulling together issues we have seen experienced by many teachers and students in our own work in US public schools.

2. For a glossary of words commonly associated with students whose first language is not English, see the "Statement of Terminology and Glossary" in the front matter of this book.

3. Some teachers, linguists, and literacy scholars use the terms *genre* and *text type* interchangeably, while others use both *genre* and *language functions* to refer to a core set of generic social processes such as describing, explaining, instructing, arguing, and narrating.

4. Source text: "Why the Bananas Belong to the Monkey" in *Fairy Tales from Brazil*, by Elsie Spicer Eells (see https://www.gutenberg.org/files/24714/24714-h/24714-h.htm#XII).

5. Some resources for writing language objectives refer to verbs that direct writers to a particular way of thinking about the task as "language functions" (Himmel, 2012). These verbs indicate that students should, for example, *identify* main ideas or *predict* what happens next. Because SFL considers all language to be functional, we avoid calling these verbs "language functions." Nevertheless, you should consider what processes the verbs in a task are asking students to do and what language objectives will focus on helping students learn the language they need to carry out such tasks.

6. Teachers in this book found the following resource helpful as they planned their lessons: *Academic Conversations: Classroom Talk That Fosters Critical Thinking and Content Understandings* (Zwiers & Crawford, 2011).

7. We don't have room in this book to define and operationalize the many grammar concepts and metalanguage terms used in SFL. Please refer to the recommended resources discussed in Chapter 7 and the annotated bibliography if you want to learn more.

8. Usually restaurants will donate unused containers if you explain they are for a classroom project.

9. This process may take more than one day to complete depending on the complexity of the texts.

10. Though not a timed test, students were expected to complete the CAHSEE English test during a single school day.

11. As of this writing, however, many states are now eliminating their high school exit exams as a response to research showing that the tests have not proved successful.

12. Sources for released writing tasks:

Arizona AIMS: http://tempeschoolsconnolly.ss3.sharpschool.com/UserFiles/Servers/Server_762372/File/Staff/Grade7Voice.pdf

California CAHSEE: http://www.cde.ca.gov/ta/tg/hs/documents/ela08rtq.pdf

New York Regents Examination: http://www.nysedregents.org/comprehensiveenglish/english-sampler-2010.pdf

13. We have seen teachers use other mnemonics such as TEA, TBEAR, BRACES, SOAPStone, etc., to support students in developing or structuring texts. It's important to make sure that your students have multiple opportunities to practice using the tool with adequate support in a low-stakes environment before they have to write on a test. There's also a risk that students might see them as a rigid formula that must be followed exactly. They should understand that these structures are guides, not rules, and they can adapt the structures to suit their purposes.

14. Adapted from Farnsworth & Malone, 2014, p. 86.

15. US federal law (Title III of the Elementary and Secondary Education Act) requires that schools have provisions in place for communicating with parents of English language learner students. Some states have legislation, as California does, requiring that all districts and school sites with at least a minimum number of ELL students have an English Learner Advisory Committee made up of parents of English language learner students and other interested community members.

Annotated Bibliography: Recommended Reading and Resources for Teachers

Assessment

Coombe, Christine, Keith S. Folse, and Nancy Hubley
A Practical Guide to Assessing English Language Learners.
Ann Arbor: University of Michigan Press, 2007.

This book provides teachers with an accessible introduction to testing each of the four language skills, as well as advice on how to develop assessments that allow students to show what they know.

Farnsworth, Timothy L., and Margaret E. Malone
Assessing English Learners in U.S. Schools.
Alexandria, VA: TESOL Press, 2014.

This easy-to-read book provides some foundational pointers for teachers unfamiliar with ways of differentiating assessment procedures to be fair for English learners. It includes several model rubrics for varying language levels.

Filkins, Scott
"Making the Reading Process Visible through Performance Assessment."
ReadWriteThink, 2012.
(http://www.readwritethink.org/professional-development/strategy-guides/making-reading-process-visible-30961.html#strategy-practice)

This strategy guide provides step-by-step instructions and reproducible resources for creating reading performance assessments suitable for ELLs.

Gottlieb, Margo
Assessing English Language Learners: Bridges to Educational Equity: Connecting Academic Language Proficiency to Student Achievement (2nd ed.).

Thousand Oaks, CA: Corwin, 2016.

This book provides in-depth resources for writing language objectives, conducting formative assessment, and addressing results from standardized tests with administrators, among other valuable topics related to assessment. Gottlieb maintains a focus on the role of equity in assessment throughout the book and also connects language assessment and the Common Core State Standards.

Kopriva, Rebecca
Ensuring Accuracy in Testing for English Language Learners.
Washington, DC: Council of Chief State School Officers, 2000.
(free download from http://files.eric.ed.gov/fulltext/ED454703.pdf)

This report provides an overview of issues related to assessment of English language learners, including how to develop test specifications that align to standards, how to write items, and how to develop rubrics that maximize fairness for ELLs. Kopriva lists accommodations that could be used to provide ELLs fair access to tests.

Genre-Based Instruction

Brisk, Maria E.
Engaging Students in Academic Literacies: Genre-Based Pedagogy for K–5 Classrooms.
New York: Routledge, 2015.

Brisk provides a clear introduction to the SFL teaching and learning cycle for examining and creating texts within specific genres, which progresses systematically from text analysis to writing. She explains the core concepts of SFL and makes connections between the text types of the Common Core State Standards and text genres taught in school. Though written for elementary teachers, the activities can easily be modified for middle and high school classes.

Mora-Flores, Eugenia
Writing Instruction for English Learners: A Focus on Genre.
Thousand Oaks, CA: Corwin Press, 2008.

This book is mainly intended for late elementary and middle school writing instruction, although many of the reproducible graphic organizers would be useful for high school writers as well. It is organized by general text type (persuasive, narrative, expository), but each chapter delves deeper into the different genres that use that text type.

O'Dowd, Elizabeth
"Finding a Voice for Argument in ELT."
TESOL Connections (2015, November).

http://newsmanager.commpartners.com/tesolc/issues/2015-11-01/2.html
This article describes how to scaffold students' discovery of the grammar of modality using an SFL approach to teaching the genre of argument writing. Each step is clearly illustrated with specific examples that could be used in teaching.

Language Analysis and SFL

Academic Language Development Network
(http://aldnetwork.org/)

This website provides "research-based teaching and assessment practices for developing the complex academic language, literacy, and thinking skills that support the learning of the Common Core State Standards, Next Generation Science Standards, ELD, and other new standards." Resources include research-based articles and teaching practice supports, as well as videos explaining academic language, language complexity, and exemplar lesson and unit plans for teaching academic language and writing language objectives.

de Oliveira, Luciana C., and Mary J. Schleppegrell
Focus on Grammar and Meaning.
Oxford, UK: Oxford University Press, 2015.

This book reviews the research on school-based academic language teaching and presents recommendations for how teachers can use SFL as an integral part of teaching multilingual students in grades K–12. Although the book mainly presents information about grammar and language, it also includes teaching ideas and activities that you can adapt to your individual teaching context and students.

Gibbons, Pauline
Scaffolding Language, Scaffolding Learning: Teaching English Language Learners in the Mainstream Classroom (2nd ed.).
Portsmouth, NH: Heinemann, 2015.

This book provides an accessible explanation of how language works in all four modalities (speaking, reading, writing, and listening). Gibbons uses SFL and copious student examples to demonstrate how teachers can make language explicit and scaffold ELLs' academic language development. The new edition has an added chapter on collaborative and group learning and one on integrating language into content teaching.

Graff, Gerald, Cathy Birkenstein, and Russel Durst
"They Say / I Say": The Moves That Matter in Academic Writing with Readings (3rd ed.).
New York: W.W. Norton, 2014.

Although this book is intended as a college writing textbook, it can also serve as a resource for teachers helping students recognize the linguistic structures writers employ in academic texts. The book is divided into sections that focus on how to report other writers' ideas and how to report one's own ideas in relation to other texts. It's important, however, to make sure that you help students analyze how language is used in these various situations rather than presenting the sentences as fill-in-the-blank formulas.

Understanding Language

(http://ell.stanford.edu/)

This website was created by a coalition of researchers "developing open-source teaching resources that support language development and learning in the content areas." The site includes research briefs, teaching resources, videos, and other resources for working with ELLs in mainstream classes, particularly with respect to the Common Core State Standards.

Communicating with Colleagues, Administrators, Families, and the Community

¡Colorín colorado!

(http://www.colorincolorado.org)

This website includes information for teachers on identification, assessment, and instruction for ELLs. The site also has sections for administrators and families of bilingual learners, as well as a section specifically about the Common Core State Standards and English language learners.

ESCORT

The Help! Kit: A Resource Guide for Secondary Teachers of Migrant English Language Learners.
Oneonta: State University of New York, 2001. (free download at http://escort.org/files/HSc1c12 .pdf)

This is a book-length report with useful resources for teachers, including guidelines for collaboration with content area teachers, a review of second language learning theory, and recommendations for ways to support families and community outreach.

National Education Association
All In! How Educators Can Advocate for English Language Learners.
Washington, DC: National Education Association, 2015.

(free download at https://www.nea.org/assets/ docs/17440_ELL_AdvocacyGuide2015_web.pdf) This book-length report is a useful tool kit for classroom teachers that outlines appropriate procedures and recommends resources for advocating for ELL students, both with school administration and with the larger community.

Pawan, Faridah, and Ginger B. Sietman, editors
Helping English Language Learners Succeed in Middle and High Schools.
Alexandria, VA: TESOL, 2007.

This collection of resources describes ways that classroom teachers and ESL specialists can collaborate to support ELL students' academic and social success in secondary schools. The authors illustrate ways that teachers and specialists in real schools have worked together; each chapter provides resources and recommendations.

References

Abedi, J. (2006). Psychometric issues in the ELL assessment and special education eligibility. *Teachers College Record, 108*(11), 2282–2303.

Abedi, J. (2010). Linguistic factors in the assessment of English learners. In G. Walford, E. Tucker, & M. Viswanathan (Eds.), *The SAGE handbook of measurement* (pp. 129–49). Los Angeles: SAGE.

Abedi, J., & Gándara, P. (2006). Performance of English language learners as a subgroup in large-scale assessment: Interaction of research and policy. *Educational Measurement: Issues and Practice, 25*(4), 36–46.

Ada, A. F., & Campoy, F. I. (2004). *Authors in the classroom: A transformative education practice.* Boston: Allyn and Bacon.

Anson, C. M. (2008). Closed systems and standardized writing tests. *College Composition and Communication, 60*(1), 113–28.

Applebee, A. N., & Langer, J. A. (2009). What is happening in the teaching of writing? *English Journal, 98*(5), 18–28.

Bailey, A. L., & Carroll, P. E. (2015). Assessment of English language learners in the era of new academic content standards. *Review of Research in Education, 39*(1), 253–94. doi:10.3102/0091732X14556074

Banks, J. A., & Banks, C. A. M. (1995). Equity pedagogy: An essential component of multicultural education. *Theory into Practice, 34*(3), 152–58.

Bean, J. C., Chappell, V. A., & Gillam, A. M. (2014). *Reading rhetorically.* Boston: Pearson.

Beers, K., & Probst, R. E. (2013). *Notice & note: Strategies for close reading.* Portsmouth, NH: Heinemann.

Black, P., & Wiliam, D. (1998). Inside the black box: Raising standards through classroom assessment. *Phi Delta Kappan, 80*(2), 139–48.

Brisk, M. E. (2015). *Engaging students in academic literacies: Genre-based pedagogy for K–5 classrooms.* New York: Routledge.

Carnock, J. T. (2015, December 4). Accountability for recently arrived ELLs: What's fair. *EdCentral.* Retrieved from http://www.edcentral.org/recent-ells-accountability/

Casanave, C. P. (2004). *Controversies in second language writing: Dilemmas and decisions in research and instruction.* Ann Arbor: University of Michigan Press.

Chokshi, S., & Fernandez, C. (2004). Challenges to importing Japanese lesson study: Concerns, misconceptions, and nuances. *Phi Delta Kappan, 85*(7), 520–25.

Coombe, C., Folse, K. S., & Hubley, N. J. (2007). *A practical guide to assessing English language learners.* Ann Arbor: University of Michigan Press.

Dare, B. (2010). Learning about language: The role of metalanguage. *NALDIC Quarterly, 8*(1), 18–25.

Darling-Hammond, L. (2006). Constructing 21st-century teacher education. *Journal of Teacher Education, 57*(3), 300–314.

Darling-Hammond, L., Wei, R. C., Andree, A., Richardson, N., & Orphanos, S. (2009). *Professional learning in the learning profession: A status report on teacher development in the United States and abroad.* Dallas: National Staff Development Council.

Delpit, L. D. (1988). The silenced dialogue: Power and pedagogy in educating other people's children. *Harvard Educational Review, 58*(3), 280–98. doi:10.17763/haer.58.3.c43481778r528qw4

de Oliveira, L. C., & Schleppegrell, M. J. (2015). *Focus on grammar and meaning.* Oxford, UK: Oxford University Press.

Derewianka, B., & Jones, P. (2010). From traditional grammar to functional grammar: Bridging the divide. *NALDIC Quarterly, 8*(1), 6–12.

Enright, K. A., & Gilliland, B. (2011). Multilingual writing in an age of accountability: From policy to practice in U.S. high school classrooms. *Journal of Second Language Writing, 20*(3), 182–95. doi:10.1016/j.jslw.2011.05.006

Every Student Succeeds Act, S. 1177, Pub. L. No. 114-95 (2015).

Fang, Z., & Schleppegrell, M. (2008). *Reading in secondary content areas: A language-based pedagogy.* Ann Arbor: University of Michigan Press.

Farnsworth, T., & Malone, M. (2014). *Assessing English learners in U.S. schools.* Alexandria, VA: TESOL Press.

Fernandez, C., & Chokshi, S. (2002). A practical guide to translating lesson study for a U.S. setting. *Phi Delta Kappan, 84*(2), 128–34.

Gibbons, P. (2002). *Scaffolding language, scaffolding learning: Teaching second language learners in the mainstream classroom.* Portsmouth, NH: Heinemann.

Gibbons, P. (2009). *English learners, academic literacy, and thinking: Learning in the challenge zone.* Portsmouth, NH: Heinemann.

Gibbons, P. (2015). *Scaffolding language, scaffolding learning: Teaching English language learners in the mainstream classroom* (2nd ed.). Portsmouth, NH: Heinemann.

Gilliland, B. (2017). Opportunity gaps: Curricular discontinuities across ESL, mainstream, and college English. In C. Ortmeier-Hooper & T. Ruecker (Eds.), *Linguistically diverse immigrant and resident writers: Transitions from high school to college* (pp. 21–35). New York: Routledge.

Gilliland, E. A. (2012). *Talking about writing: Culturally and linguistically diverse adolescents' socialization into academic literacy* (Unpublished doctoral dissertation). University of California, Davis.

Giouroukakis, V., & Honigsfeld, A. (2010). High-stakes testing and English language learners: Using culturally and linguistically responsive literacy practices in the high school English classroom. *TESOL Journal, 1*(4), 470–99.

Goals 2000: Educate America Act, H.R. 1804 (1994).

Goldenberg, C., & Coleman, R. (2010). *Promoting academic achievement among English learners: A guide to the research.* Thousand Oaks, CA: Corwin.

Hammond, J. (2006). High challenge, high support: Integrating language and content instruction for diverse learners in an English literature classroom. *Journal of English for Academic Purposes, 5*(4), 269–83.

Hillocks, G., Jr. (2002). *The testing trap: How state writing assessments control learning.* New York: Teachers College Press.

Hillocks, G., Jr. (2003). How state assessments lead to vacuous thinking and writing. *Journal of Writing Assessment, 1*(1), 5–21.

Hillocks, G., Jr. (2011). *Teaching argument writing, grades 6–12: Supporting claims with relevant evidence and clear reasoning.* Portsmouth, NH: Heinemann.

Himmel, J. (2012). Language objectives: The key to effective content area instruction for English learners. *¡Colorín colorado!* Retrieved from http://www.colorincolorado.org/article/language-objectives-key-effective-content-area-instruction-english-learners

Hinkel, E. (2015). *Effective curriculum for teaching L2 writing: Principles and techniques.* New York: Taylor & Francis.

Hyland, K. (2003). *Second language writing.* Cambridge, UK: Cambridge University Press.

Johns, A. M. (1997). *Text, role, and context: Developing academic literacies.* Cambridge, UK: Cambridge University Press.

Johns, A. M. (2011). The future of genre in L2 writing: Fundamental, but contested, instructional decisions. *Journal of Second Language Writing, 20*(1), 56–68. doi:10.1016/j.jslw.2010.12.003

Jones, B. D., & Egley, R. J. (2007). Learning to take tests or learning for understanding? Teachers' beliefs about test-based accountability. *The Educational Forum, 71*(3), 232–48. doi:10.1080/00131720709335008

Jones, M. G., Jones, B. D., & Hargrove, T. Y. (2003). *The unintended consequences of high-stakes testing.* Lanham, MD: Rowman & Littlefield.

Klein, A. (2015, November 30). ESEA reauthorization: The Every Student Succeeds Act explained. *Education Week.* Retrieved from http://blogs.edweek.org/edweek/campaign-k-12/2015/11/esea_reauthorization_the_every.html

Kopriva, R. (2000). *Ensuring accuracy in testing for English language learners.* Washington, DC: Council of Chief State School Officers.

Lattimer, H. (2003). *Thinking through genre: Units of study in reading and writing workshops 4–12.* Portland, ME: Stenhouse.

Levine, T. H., & Bunch, G. C. (2007). Community: Collaborating to develop partnerships with parents and the wider school community. In F.

Pawan & G. B. Sietman (Eds.), *Helping English language learners succeed in middle and high schools* (pp. 117–40). Alexandria, VA: TESOL.

Lewis, C. (2002). Does lesson study have a future in the United States? *Nagoya Journal of Education and Human Development, 3*(1), 1–23.

Lewis, C. C., Perry, R. R., Friedkin, S., & Roth, J. R. (2012). Improving teaching does improve teachers: Evidence from lesson study. *Journal of Teacher Education, 63*(5), 368–75. doi:10.1177/0022487112446633

Lindahl, K., & Watkins, N. M. (2014). What's on the "LO" menu? Supporting academic language objective development. *The Clearing House: A Journal of Educational Strategies, Issues and Ideas, 87*(5), 197–203. doi:10.1080/00098655.2014.918531

Marrongelle, K., Sztajn, P., & Smith, M. (2013). Scaling up professional development in an era of common state standards. *Journal of Teacher Education, 64*(3), 202–11. doi:10.1177/0022487112473838

Martin, J. R. (1997). Analysing genre: Functional parameters. In F. Christie & J. R. Martin (Eds.), *Genres and institutions: Social processes in the workplace and school* (pp. 3–39). London: Cassell.

Martin, J. R., & Rose, D. (2007). *Working with discourse: Meaning beyond the clause* (2nd ed.). London: Continuum.

Menken, K. (2006). Teaching to the test: How No Child Left Behind impacts language policy, curriculum, and instruction for English language learners. *Bilingual Research Journal, 30*(2), 521–46.

Menken, K. (2008). *English learners left behind: Standardized testing as language policy.* Clevedon, UK: Multilingual Matters.

Menken, K. (2010). NCLB and English language learners: Challenges and consequences. *Theory into Practice, 49*(2), 121–28.

Moore, J., & Schleppegrell, M. (2014). Using a functional linguistics metalanguage to support academic language development in the English Language Arts. *Linguistics and Education, 26*, 92–105. doi:10.1016/j.linged.2014.01.002

Mora-Flores, E. (2008). *Writing instruction for English learners: A focus on genre.* Thousand Oaks, CA: Corwin Press.

No Child Left Behind (Elementary and Secondary Education Act), Pub. L. No. 107-110 (2001).

O'Hara, S., Pritchard, R., Huang, C., & Pella, S. (2013a). Learning to integrate new technologies into teaching and learning through a design-based model of professional development. *Journal of Technology and Teacher Education, 21*(2), 203–23.

O'Hara, S., Pritchard, R., Huang, C., & Pella, S. (2013b). The teaching using technology studio: Innovative professional development to meet the needs of English learners. *TESOL Journal, 4*(2), 274–94.

Olsen, L. (2010). *Reparable harm: Fulfilling the unkept promise of educational opportunity for California's long term English learners.* Long Beach, CA: Californians Together.

Paltridge, B. (2001). *Genre and the language learning classroom.* Ann Arbor: University of Michigan Press.

Patthey, G., Thomas-Spiegel, J., & Dillon, P. (2009). Educational pathways of Generation 1.5 students in community college writing courses. In M. M. Roberge, M. Siegal & L. Harklau (Eds.), *Generation 1.5 in college composition: Teaching academic writing to U.S.-educated learners of ESL* (pp. 135–49). New York: Routledge.

Pella, S. (2011). A situative perspective on developing writing pedagogy in a teacher professional learning community. *Teacher Education Quarterly, 38*(1), 107–25.

Pella, S. (2012). What should count as data for data-driven instruction? Toward contextualized data-inquiry models for teacher education and professional development. *Middle Grades Research Journal, 7*(1), 57–75.

Pella, S. (2015a). Learning to teach writing in the age of standardization and accountability: Toward an equity writing pedagogy. *Journal of Writing Teacher Education, 4*(1). Retrieved from http://scholarworks.wmich.edu/wte/vol4/iss1/1

Pella, S. (2015b). Pedagogical reasoning and action; Affordances of practice-based teacher professional development. *Teacher Education Quarterly, 42*(3), 81–99.

Plank, S. B., & Condliffe, B. F. (2013). Pressures of the season: An examination of classroom quality and high-stakes accountability. *American*

Educational Research Journal, 50(5), 1152–82. doi:10.3102/0002831213500691

Probst, R. (1994). Reader-response theory and the English curriculum. *English Journal, 83*(3), 37–44.

Ramanathan, V., & Atkinson, D. (1999). Individualism, academic writing, and ESL writers. *Journal of Second Language Writing, 8*(1), 45–75. doi:10.1016/S1060-3743(99)80112-X

Robertson, K. (2007). Bilingual family night for ELL families. *¡Colorín colorado!* Retrieved from http://www.colorincolorado.org/article/bilingual-family-night-ell-families

Russikoff, K. A. (2013). FRIEDS: A development device. In D. C. Mussman (Ed.), *New ways in teaching writing* (pp. 26–28). Alexandria, VA: TESOL International Association.

Sadler, D. R. (1989). Formative assessment and the design of instructional systems. *Instructional Science, 18*(2), 119–44.

Sandberg, K. L., & Reschly, A. L. (2011). English learners: Challenges in assessment and the promise of curriculum-based measurement. *Remedial and Special Education, 32*(2), 144–54. doi:10.1177/0741932510361260

Schleppegrell, M. (2004). *The language of schooling: A functional linguistics perspective*. Mahwah, NJ: Lawrence Erlbaum.

Schleppegrell, M. (2010). Supporting a "reading to write" pedagogy with functional grammar. *NALDIC Quarterly, 8*(1), 26–31.

Schleppegrell, M., Greer, S., & Taylor, S. (2008). Literacy in history: Language and meaning. *Australian Journal of Language and Literacy, 31*(2), 174–87.

Schleppegrell, M., & O'Hallaron, C. L. (2011). Teaching academic language in L2 secondary settings. *Annual Review of Applied Linguistics, 31*, 3–18. doi:10.1017/s0267190511000067

Shaul, M. S., & Ganson, H. C. (2005). The No Child Left Behind Act of 2001: The federal government's role in strengthening accountability for student performance. *Review of Research in Education, 29*, 151–54. doi:10.3102/0091732X029001151

Shohamy, E. (2006). *Language policy: Hidden agendas and new approaches*. London: Routledge.

Smagorinsky, P. (2008). *Teaching English by design: How to create and carry out instructional units*. Portsmouth, NH: Heinemann.

Solano-Flores, G., & Trumbull, E. (2003). Examining language in context: The need for new research and practice paradigms in the testing of English-language learners. *Educational Researcher, 32*(2), 3–13.

Solórzano, R. W. (2008). High stakes testing: Issues, implications, and remedies for English language learners. *Review of Educational Research, 78*(2), 260–329. doi:http://dx.doi.org/10.3102/0034654308317845

Spycher, P. (2007). Academic writing of adolescent English learners: Learning to use "although." *Journal of Second Language Writing, 16*(4), 238–54. doi:10.1016/j.jslw.2007.07.001

Stanford Center for Assessment, Learning, & Equity (2016). Making good choices: A support guide for edTPA candidates. Retrieved from https://www.edtpa.com/Content/Docs/edTPAMGC.pdf

Student Achievement Partners. (2015). *Introduction to the ELA / literacy shifts* [professional development module]. Retrieved from http://achievethecore.org/page/394/professional-development-introduction-to-the-ela-literacy-shifts

Sullivan, A. L. (2011). Disproportionality in special education identification and placement of English language learners. *Exceptional Children, 77*(3), 317–34.

TESOL International Association. (2013, March). *Overview of the Common Core State Standards initiatives for ELLs*. Alexandria, VA: TESOL International Association.

Valdés, G., Kibler, A., & Walqui, A. (2014). *Changes in the expertise of ESL professionals: Knowledge and action in an era of new standards*. Alexandria, VA: TESOL International Association.

Wiggins, G., & McTighe, J. (2011). *The understanding by design guide to creating high-quality units*. Alexandria, VA: ASCD.

Zwiers, J., & Crawford, M. (2011) *Academic conversations: Classroom talk that fosters critical thinking and content understandings*. Portland, ME: Stenhouse.

Index

Authors

Photo by Bob Brewer

Betsy Gilliland is an assistant professor in the Department of Second Language Studies at the University of Hawaiʻi Mānoa, where she teaches courses in second language teaching and learning, adolescent second language literacy, and action research. Her research and publications examine high school teachers' work with immigrant second language writers and language teachers' development of inquiry research methods. She holds a PhD in education from the University of California, Davis, and an MA in TESOL with a Vermont K–12 ESL teaching credential from the SIT Graduate Institute. Gilliland has taught Russian and English as a second or foreign language to children and adults in the United States, Thailand, and Uzbekistan, and taught developmental and college writing in California.

Shannon Pella is an assistant professor in the College of Education at California State University, Sacramento, where she teaches courses in English language development and disciplinary literacy in the single subject teaching credentials program. Her research and publications examine pedagogical reasoning and shifts in perspectives and practices as teachers engage in collaborative, inquiry-oriented, and practice-based professional learning. She holds a PhD in education from the University of California, Davis, an MA in social sciences, and two California teaching credentials. Pella has taught secondary ELD, English, and history and supports teacher collaboration and professional development across the disciplines at John F. Kennedy High School in Sacramento, California.

This book was typeset in Janson Text and BotonBQ by
Barbara Frazier.

Typefaces used on the cover include American Typewriter,
Frutiger, and Formata.

The book was printed on 60-lb. White Recycled Offset paper
by Versa Press, Inc.

30% Total Recycled Fiber